Chocolate Malts & Nickel Sodas

Chocolate Malts & Nickel Sodas

MARGARET JOHNSON

ZONDERVAN
PUBLISHING HOUSE
OF THE ZONDERVAN CORPORATION | GRAND RAPIDS, MICHIGAN 49506

Some of the names and places have been altered to protect the privacy of the individuals involved.

CHOCOLATE MALTS AND NICKEL SODAS
© 1976 by The Zondervan Corporation
Grand Rapids, Michigan

Second edition 1978

Library of Congress Cataloging in Publication Data

Johnson, Margaret.
    Chocolate malts and nickel sodas

    1. Johnson, Margaret.   I. Title.
CT275.J6777A29   973.91'092'4 [B]   76-10627

ISBN 0-310-26661-0

Printed in the United States of America

To my husband, VERN, who made all my dreams come true. Through all the years his tender strength and cherishing love have been constant.

To our children, CINDY, RICH, DAVE, DAN, and in loving memory of KATHI "so dear to our hearts." They have enriched our home and our lives beyond words.

And to MY MOTHER, who taught us the true meaning of courage in her hour of testing.

My thanks to my son Dave for first reading the manuscript nodding his eighteen-year-old approval, and encouraging me to "get on with it" whenever I set it aside.

I am grateful also to Peggy Wilson for spending long hours reading those pages, offering helpful suggestions, and expertly typing the manuscript from rough draft into final copy.

I also wish to acknowledge all of those who touched my life during the years of "Chocolate Malts and Nickel Sodas." Though their names have been changed, they know who they are, and my gratitude is deep. I give special tribute of love and thanks to "Nancy and Jennifer" for opening the door to "a better way" and walking along that way with me in a joyous friendship that is still fresh and glowing today.

When my world is particularly pleasant and good,
And friends are warm and loving,
And all is well with my world,
Then, Lord, give me pause to think
Of the cares of others.
Amidst my fulfilled life style,
Let me see the hurting heart
And care.

When I'm praising you, Lord,
For my joy-filled life,
Give me a jolt so I'll stop to consider
The despairing one.
I once lived there in that land of nothing.
Let me remember the emptiness
And care.

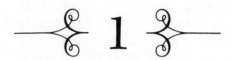

1

The ten o'clock warning bell had already sounded, and the halls were emptying of students. If I didn't hurry, I would be late for class. But even from the musty corridors I could see the sunshine of the fresh June morning as it filtered through the huge classroom windows, beckoning me away from the stuffy rooms out into the dazzling sunlight.

If I had thought of it earlier, I would have tried to find the gang before school, and we could have escaped to the lake; but it was too late now. I quickened my pace and headed for my third-period class. The door was ajar and students were already settling into their seats when I heard someone call my name. As I turned, Kate almost ran into me. I juggled my books to keep them from falling.

Kate was breathless, peering around me at the partially filled classroom. "Imagine French class on a day like this," she grimaced. "I've already rounded up the gang. Hurry and get the car. We'll meet you at the corner."

Then she was gone, dashing through the crowd of teen-agers who were scurrying for their classrooms. Hesitating for just a fraction of a second, I made a sharp turn and hurried through the vast corridors out the wide doors, down the steps, and into my late-model Plymouth convertible.

Kate could talk me into anything, although on such a warm day it didn't take much to convince me that the call of the outdoors was more alluring than old Mr. Caron droning on in his high-pitched, professional French. He rambled on almost as if there were no students seated before him. The boredom on our faces escaped his oblivious eyes as he turned to scrawl foreign words on the wall-to-wall blackboard.

The fresh morning air caught my breath and lifted my spirits as I maneuvered my car out of the parking lot. To escape even one hour of that boring French class was enough to ease my worry about an excuse for tomorrow.

It was my boyfriend Tom I really wanted to see, and for one anxious moment I wondered if Kate had managed to find him. But my fears proved ungrounded, for just as the sharp ringing of the bell pronounced class in session, my friends emerged, running and laughing, quickly lengthening the gap between themselves and the school. They piled into my car, throwing their schoolbooks carelessly on the floor. Kate, Rick, Marie, Sherry, Johnny, and Tom, all talking at once as they related their narrow escapes in racing past the monitors and out the doors.

As I headed my car away from the narrow residential streets toward the highway leading to Green Lake, we all breathed a sigh of relief. The top of my convertible was down, letting the cool breeze sweep through our hair and caress our faces. At first the noise of the city competed with our shouts, but then the business of the main streets was receding, and soon we would be under the shade of towering elm trees.

Green Lake was a sparkling jewel set far back from the main road, nearly hidden by the shade trees that abundantly surrounded its shores. The water, calm and warmly blue on hot summer days, turned a pale green in the evening under clear skies and a softly reflecting moon.

Now we were rounding the bend, and the quiet of the narrow dirt road was interrupted only by our shrieks as the guys stood up to pull low hanging branches from trees bending like a sheltering arc over the graveled lane.

Scrambling from the car, we ran toward the pavilion,

confident that this early in June there would be few people around. What a contrast to the hot July days, when the sun-drenched porch surrounding the pavilion would be crowded with barefoot bathers, ice-cream cones dripping, racing across the wooden deck.

We leaned over the counter and ordered hamburgers and cokes. And while the others left to spread their food on nearby picnic tables, Tom and I lingered on the porch, sitting at a small table overlooking the beauty of the pale blue water.

At first neither of us spoke. The silence of the morning and the intangible loveliness of simply being together was enough. We watched the soft waters lapping around the aging wooden pier. Old, weather-beaten rowboats tied to the dock bobbed in rhythm to the ebb and flow of the waters.

Tom lighted a cigarette and inhaled deeply. The look on his face told me he was about to say something I didn't want to hear. I playfully brushed my lips against his cheek hoping to bring a lightness to his somber mood.

"Sure beats French class," I laughed.

Tom turned to face me. "When is this all going to stop, Margaret?" When he called me by my full name, I knew he was serious. Usually it was a teasing "Maggie" or "Marge" or a tender "sweetheart." But now he was looking at me intently, expecting an answer. I made a big thing of sipping my Coke until he pulled the straw from my mouth.

"You're not only going to flunk French, but all of your classes. What's wrong with you anyway?"

If I could have answered his question, it might have prevented some of my future heartache. But I honestly didn't know what "was wrong" with me. We fell into an uncomfortable silence until Tom took my hand. The lecture was not over yet.

"You're letting Kate run your life. You always have. If you don't stop skipping school, you won't be passing your finals. Have you thought of that?"

"It doesn't matter, Tom," I sighed. Sailboats in the distance, bobbing in the rippling waters, were capturing my attention. I imagined that Tom and I were sailing together, and in a moment we would drift beyond the horizon and disappear into another world. But Tom interrupted my reverie as he spoke gruffly.

"What does that mean? Of course it matters. A girl like you with money and a family who cares — how can you say it doesn't matter?" His voice grew tender. "Marge, will you please look at me?"

I turned to look into Tom's golden-flecked eyes, and as always my heart skipped a little remembering the first time I had ever seen him. It was the previous fall at the beginning of my freshman year. My English teacher wanted me to read an essay I had written before the junior-senior English class. I was reading aloud when I glanced up and found myself looking into smiling brown eyes, flecked with tiny golden specks. My hands began to shake, and my voice did funny things. Our eyes met for a moment, just like in the movies, and I thought surely the class must have heard my heart crash into captivity.

After class he waited for me and complimented me on my composition, calmly taking the books from my arms and walking along beside me in an easy stride. His name was Tom, and suddenly it became the only name in the world, singing through my mind like a sweet, unending refrain.

After that, Tom and I spent most of our lunch hours together, and after school we met at the ice-cream parlor, sitting in a corner booth surrounded by chattering kids and blaring music from the constantly flashing jukebox. We talked about school and football games and the latest recordings. Once in awhile Tom spoke briefly about his stepfather, with an edge to his voice that warned me not to ask too much about his home life.

That was fine with me because I didn't want to tell him much about mine either. He only knew that I lived in an elegant, sprawling brick house on the edge of town, and he was painfully aware that I had my own car and charge accounts at all the best department stores.

I guess money was important to Tom, but I wished I

could tell him that money couldn't buy happiness or satisfy the restlessness that ached inside me. I didn't tell him that my parents were religious and kept long lists of do's and dont's that would seem laughable and far removed from the world we knew.

My three older brothers were out of the house now, two married and one dead. I never told him that our home, which had once been peaceful, had become hectic after my brother Barry's death. His only child, a helpless invalid, had been left in my parents' care. This dark-haired little girl, crippled from birth, had blown into my life like a whirling, unwanted wind, shattering the tranquillity of our home. How could I ever explain to Tom what I felt deep inside toward this helpless child? He couldn't comprehend something I couldn't even explain. My resentment deepened every day at the way fate had decided to turn my life around.

I had every right to my resentment, I reasoned, and I hugged it close, using it to protect myself against unanswered questions. For instance, if God was so good, as my father insisted, why did He let my favorite brother die and leave behind a crippled child? To me God seemed like a dictator waiting for someone to get out of line so He could quickly zap him back into place. Or sometimes I wondered if He watched carefully to see what made a person the happiest so He could snatch away the pleasure.

Everything I enjoyed was taboo in our home. My world of swinging music, movies, and dancing all met with disapproval from my father who, in my mind, had become just like the God he always talked about. I couldn't understand, and I told myself it no longer mattered.

I allowed Tom to see only the lighthearted girl, the butterfly who had escaped the cocoon. I never hinted that beneath the surface were many searching questions which were better left unasked and unanswered.

But now I was becoming angry with Tom. He was getting as bad as my father, always criticizing Kate. I frowned, pulling my hand away.

"Kate's my best friend, Tom. Leave her alone."

"If she were a good friend, she wouldn't talk you into skipping school and a lot of other things you know you shouldn't be doing."

We sat in silence for awhile watching a tiny gull settle precariously on the water. Finally I sighed, "I wish I could stay here forever."

Tom put his arm around my shoulder, and I leaned hard against him. "Okay, Marge, I won't talk about it anymore. But will you promise me something?"

I looked up into his serious eyes and waited, wondering what he was going to say.

"After I'm gone, will you promise me that you'll finish school? Even if it means changing schools and making a fresh start for yourself, will you promise you'll be good and graduate?"

After I'm gone, were the only words I heard.

"Gone where?" I straightened up and whispered, my heart pounding. Tom was the only part of my life that really mattered. If he wasn't there, life wouldn't be worth living at all.

"Now listen — ", Tom was speaking gently as though I were a little child, "there's going to be a war very soon — and when it happens, I'm enlisting. It's something I'll have to do. You understand that, don't you?"

"No," I caught a small, quick breath. "I don't understand, and who says there's going to be a war?"

"Just believe me," he said quietly. "You don't think the United States is going to let Hitler take over the whole world, do you? He's gone far enough already. We have to stop him, and it won't be long before we're in it just like England."

Hitler? That marching, screaming madman in Germany? But what in the world did he have to do with Tom and me? He was oceans away. And who cared about what went on in the rest of the world anyway?

Tom, so gentle for a boy not yet eighteen, brushed the hot tears that were gathering on my eyelashes. Words tried to escape, but my lips were trembling so I couldn't speak.

Finally Tom said comfortingly, "It's not going to happen this afternoon, you know, but promise me anyway."

"I promise," I mumbled, not caring what I was promising. How could I go on if Tom should leave me? That was one promise I had no intention of keeping, because somehow I just knew I could keep Tom from enlisting. With that thought my spirits lifted a little, and I smiled.

"I promise, Tom," and I brushed my lips against his.

"Life isn't one continuous picnic, babe, remember that. There *will* be a war, and things will change. I just want you to be prepared."

Our friends, barefoot in the wet sand, were waving at us to join them, and we waved back as we walked hand in hand across the damp grass to the sandy shore.

We tossed pebbles as far into the lake as we could, and the stillness of the waters comforted me somehow. Of course there wouldn't be a war. Silly, worrisome Tom. And when someone suggested we go back to the pavilion and play the jukebox, I was glad.

Rick put a nickel in the nickelodeon, and we sang to the crazy tune of "Three Little Fishes." Dancing there on the wooden deck of the old pavilion, Europe seemed a planet away.

The late afternoon breeze brought with it the sweet fragrance of nearby lilac bushes mingled with the lush green grass, still fresh from the late May rains.

Our last dance was always Glenn Miller's "Moonlight Cocktail." Tom held me tenderly that spring afternoon, his lips touching my hair, not saying a word.

It all seems like a dream I had a lifetime ago, but the memory of it sweeps over me now and then. Whenever I hear an old Glenn Miller album playing the plaintive "couple of jiggers of moonlight and add a star," I remember the hot summer days and cool evenings we spent at lovely Green Lake. And then I think sadly of Tom.

We couldn't know that afternoon as we walked together up the hill to the car that this would be the last summer of our young love. That before the next summer Tom would be killed on a navy ship somewhere in the South Pacific.

As Tom took the wheel of my Plymouth and expertly drove us back through the winding dirt roads and onto the highway leading to town, I ruffled his brown curls. This was no ordinary teen-age crush. Tom and I were really in love. My whole world of happiness depended on him. I sighed and snuggled close. Nothing would ever happen to him — not now or ever.

I was as wrong that day as Tom had been right about everything else — about Kate, about me, and about the storm clouds over Europe that were about to engulf the whole world in a terrible, shattering war.

That was the way we were, we teen-agers of the prewar years. There was war in Europe casting a shadow over our own country, but we thought any real threat of danger too remote to consider. We were just beginning to feel the first waves of prosperity after the hardships of the Depression years. Even our parents were trying to avoid the gathering storm and were welcoming what to them seemed the start of a bright new world.

We had our own money to spend at Walgreen's Drugstore after school where we drank five-cent soda pop and devoured fifteen-cent sundaes laden with nuts and whipped cream. In the evening, we often went to the Savoy Theater for the best thirty-five-cent double-feature in town.

The big screen was the world of our dreams. Munching on hot, buttered popcorn, we thrilled as dashing Errol Flynn dueled his way through corridors of cement staircases to victory. We adored Tyrone Power's dark good looks and sometimes sat through his pictures twice. Some, raised in an era of poverty and despair, identified immediately with John Garfield's portrayal of the sullen born loser. But Clark Gable was the "take charge" hero who usually lived in our fantasies.

Sprawling along a short city block, Southeast High was flanked by a football field on one side and an ice-cream parlor on the other. In our favorite after-school haunt, small, round tables skirted the miniature dance floor, and the center of our world was the giant jukebox. The records spun our dreams; and when a new voice began crooning, "This love of ours," a star was born, and like girls all over the nation, we fell hopelessly in love with Frank Sinatra.

We girls wore fuzzy Sloppy Joe sweaters, sizes too large, dirty saddle shoes (much to the consternation of our mothers), and a single strand of pearls. Our curly hair was set high into pompadours or Ginger Rogers pageboys. Our fingernails were long and painted with ruby-red nail polish that exactly matched the color of our lips. Pancake make-up was coated on clean, healthy skin or applied more heavily to cover teen-age blemishes. Our final touch was lavish dabs of "Evening in Paris" cologne.

Loose-fitting tweed coats provided little barricade against the fierce winters. Often we tied colorful silk bandannas around our heads but we were either immune to the cold or just young enough to ignore it. Rolling our skirts high and walking knee-deep through drifts of snow seemed no hardship at all. Whether the snow fell swiftly, forming high drifts, or the flakes floated down lazily, winter was a time for ice-skating on frozen ponds, our freezing hands clad in thin mittens.

Spring always brought a new beginning, with its budding trees and the smell of fresh April rains. When June finally blossomed, we coined the phrase, "What is so rare as a day in school?" and took off for the lake to lie under the hot sun in absolute stillness, welcoming the warmth and promise of another summer.

Sometimes during our more serious moments we would discuss the war that was raging in Europe, but the conversation would be short, never leading to any conclusion. It usually went like this:

SHERRY: Who does Hitler think he is anyway?

JOHNNY: He's getting what he wants — half of Europe.

RICK: It's none of our business. I think we should stay out of it.

TOM: Of course it's our business. We can't let the little countries be taken over by one man.

ME: And the way he's treating the Jews.

We had seen newsreels in the movie houses of the beginnings of anti-Semitism in Germany, but we never dreamed of the real horrors of concentration camps or the mass murders of the Jewish people in those countries.

JOHNNY: Who cares about the Jews?

ME: Well — God does.

I tried to say it lightly so they wouldn't think I was hung up on God or religion, because I wasn't. I had heard my father thunder about God's judgment on those who persecuted the Jews, but secretly I was wondering why God was letting this happen. If He were God, He could stop it, couldn't He? God's ways were a sour mystery to me — a mystery I had decided not to try to unravel.

KATE: God? Hey, how did we get on this subject?

RICK: Yeah! Let's talk about something else. Who has a nickel?

And so it went. We didn't know where to carry our conversation beyond wondering and thinking. Besides, we were young, and the problems on the other side of the world seemed to have nothing whatsoever to do with us.

Rick deliberated a long time at the jukebox, until finally the sound of the "Hut Sut Song" drowned out our hidden fears.

There was nothing to worry about. Yesterday with all its despair was over. This was 1940, and we belonged to the richest and strongest country in the world. We had the wisest president, and he would know what to do. He himself had said that the only thing to fear was fear itself.

And so now to dance, to laugh, to enjoy. Sherry and Johnny, as usual, began their elaborate jitterbugging as the rest of us stood around the edge of the floor to clap them on.

There was nothing to think about except school and proms and football games and young love. Life was one big chocolate soda, and there seemed to be no end to its delicious sweetness.

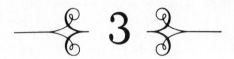

3

As a child, I couldn't think of a problem in the world that would affect me.

My childhood world was made up of tree-lined streets, open fields, and burning leaves on cool autumn evenings. Fun was jumping rope on clean, quiet sidewalks and playing marbles on the sandy playground after school. Winning shiny blue agates to carry home in a tightly tied bag was its own reward. And I still have happy memories of strolling lazily to June's Candy Store with my best friend on Saturday afternoons, tightly holding our pennies and gazing at the endless rows of candy bins, deliberating over what to buy.

On hot summer afternoons I carefully placed the card in our window for the ice man, making sure the right number was up so that he could see how many pounds of ice we needed that day for our ice box. While we children waited for the sound of his rumbling truck, we busied ourselves drawing chalk squares on the sidewalks for a game of hopscotch or sat together on long cool porches playing jacks. When at last the old van turned our corner, we jumped up, raced to the street, and watched in fascination while the powerful ice man lowered the heavy canvas, revealing at last — mountains of blocked ice. How strong and confident he handled his huge pick, carefully selecting just the right block, lifting it high on his shoulder, and carrying it into the house. When we were sure he was inside, we caught little chips of ice, holding them to our mouths and relishing the coolness in the heat of those scorching days.

In December we ice-skated on frozen ponds and went sledding on steep driveways and hills until the freezing temperatures forced us indoors, where we stood on wide floor heaters and let the ice drip from our clothes. The delicious warmth was part of the joy. Then as the seasons changed, spring-filled, cloudless days found us chasing butterflies, waving our nets as we ran through the grassy fields.

But, threaded throughout the seasons, conversation in our homes centered more and more on "hard times" and what President Roosevelt was going to do about them with his "New Deal."

The year was 1936, and the country was deep in the Depression. But there was one confident voice, familiar and comforting, heard in the land attempting to lift the spirits of the people and build trust in the future of America. When he spoke, a kind of magic filled the air. One wanted to cry and nod and desperately believe all he said.

"There is a mysterious cycle in human events. To some generations much is given. Of other generations much is expected. This generation has a rendezvous with destiny." It was Roosevelt speaking from Franklin Field just months before election day. This time his opponent was Alfred Landon.

I watched the parade of voters that November marching grimly into our grade-school gym to cast their ballots. How solemn and mysterious it all seemed, almost as though they had a secret locked tightly inside them where no child was allowed. The world of voting polls was for grown-ups, and we couldn't taste their bitter defeat or know their glory of victory.

"Do you think Landon will win?" I asked one lady as she

walked silently along the curved school sidewalk.

"I'm afraid not, honey," she answered sadly.

She was right. FDR's victory was a landslide, much to the consternation of my father, who stalked through our home bitterly denouncing "that man in the White House."

One summer afternoon I saw President Roosevelt as he rode through our town in a motorcade, waving and lifting his gray fedora. I stared after his car for a long time, hardly believing that I had seen a real president. The fact that he couldn't walk seemed to be a further tribute to his courage. To me he was a hero.

Yet there were reminders throughout the country that all was not well. Everyone was talking about the Depression that was gripping the nation. Even with the WPA and the relief program, there seemed little hope that things would ever be right again.

When one of my friends moved out of her big home into a garage made over for their family, my mother explained that times were hard, men were out of work, and money was scarce. I listened wide-eyed to talk of bread lines and bank failures. I couldn't understand any of it, for money was plentiful in our home, and life was pleasant.

I had many friends on our short block, but on a cold rainy day when none of them wanted to leave the cozy warmth of home, I would snuggle deep into the green velvet chair in our front parlor, content with a good book and the sounds of mother working in the kitchen.

I remember so well sitting on hard pews in Sunday school, swinging my legs while I memorized Scripture verses to catchy tunes. We children raced across the park at the annual church picnic, running again and again to the never-empty lemonade barrel, waiting anxiously for the call to the picnic dinner where long wooden tables were laden with delicious foods.

We swung each other high on swings until we could look straight up into the clouds, screaming partly with fear but mostly with delight. And finally, as dusk settled on the park, we climbed into our cars and were happily asleep long before we even reached the highway. It was a joyful childhood that never hinted it would ever become anything less. I believed with all my heart in the verses I learned and the songs I sang. I was certain that "Jesus loved me" and nothing would ever happen to hurt me or those I loved.

But that was the joy of an innocent child, and soon I began to realize that things *did* happen to people.

It was on a cool April afternoon that I came home from school to find my parents silent in chilled grief. Their dearest friend, my adored "Uncle Paul," our Sunday school leader for as long as I could remember, had come home from work to discover his wife and two children brutally murdered. I shivered in horror as pieces of the tragedy began to unfold. It was doubly terrifying for me because Uncle Paul's son Ronnie had been my own playmate. We had chased each other through vacant pews after church as our parents stood visiting, or we sat giggling through long church services until we felt a nudge from either side. Ronnie had been my friend, and now he was dead. I lay sleepless wondering why God had allowed such a terrible thing to happen to dear Uncle Paul's family. I felt rebellion rise against the question I didn't think could ever be answered.

My heart pounded through the funeral, my eyes never leaving the small casket that held my friend. Uncle Paul kept on talking about how near God was even in his deepest grief, and I thought how wrong it was for him to have to face such a loss. Couldn't he see that God was unfair? How could he trust a God who would do such a thing?

It took me a long time to sort out my muddled thoughts. And when finally I could reason coolly, I decided that I could never fully trust God again.

4

The autumn of my twelfth year stands out vividly in my mind because after that things were never the same, and I came to the sober realization that life would not always be pleasant and good.

Tension was heavy in our home. I felt it like an electric current until it could be hidden no longer. My eighteen-year-old brother Barry was "in trouble." The pretty blonde he had been dating was going to have his baby; and though my parents felt isolated in disgrace, Barry seemed untouched by it all.

Wedding plans were made for early December, and Barry and his bride, Sally, stood in our living room and exchanged their vows. Barry didn't seem sad at all, so why did everyone else? I wished with all my heart that he could be the happiest person in the world.

It was not to be. Almost overnight he turned from a twinkling-eyed boy into a man. If only time could turn back to when Barry was carefree, snapping his fingers to catchy tunes and doing soft-shoe dances around the house.

I remembered him at our summer cottage on beautiful Gull Lake, winning first prize in the swimming contests each year, surging far ahead of his opponents. Our family stood on the shore and shouted for him to swim faster, and when finally he pulled himself up on the shore, he stood waving his lean tan arms in victory.

It was Barry who patiently taught me how to swim. And when my strokes met with his satisfaction, he tutored me in the finer art of diving.

When the sun went down, casting a glowing red sunset over the beautiful waters and turning them a sapphire blue, Barry would expertly guide our sailboat onto the lake, gathering about him a laughing group of his friends.

Now Barry was tired, uncaring, sleeping soundlessly after work sprawled on the sofa, drawing farther and farther away from his young wife — from all of us — into a world of his own.

When we visited their apartment, I tried to pretend that nothing had changed. But when I talked to Barry, he looked away with disinterest until I could think of nothing more to say. He became silent and withdrawn.

My memories of Barry as he had been were an obsession, and I began to realize that people and circumstances did change and were never the same again.

Barry and Sally's baby was born in the spring, long before she was due. They named her April. What a perfect name for this little girl who would grow to be as lovely as the month that had just arrived, bringing with it sweet fragrances and colorful flowers.

Standing at the hospital nursery window with my mother, staring at the tiny baby lying so still in the incubator, I thought to myself, *Everything will be all right now*. Soon the baby would go home to be with her parents, and our home would know the peace and tranquillity that had escaped it for the past several months.

But everything was not all right. Something had gone terribly wrong. The three doctors in the small hospital room soberly describing April's difficulty sent a cold terror through me. "Perhaps it was because she was born too soon," one doctor offered. "Hopefully her mind and speech will be undamaged." Only time would tell, they sighed, and quickly left the room.

No one spoke. No one could. Sally lay sobbing quietly, and Barry was stunned. All traces of boyishness were gone from his handsome face. My parents were dejected in their helplessness. I wanted to run from that desolate room and never look back.

In the summer little April went home to her parents. We visited their apartment often, and my mother always hurried to hold the tiny child, to feed her, to encourage any slight improvement. We always left with my mother in tears, not bothering to wipe them away as they slid down her cheeks.

But the hardest part for me was watching Barry as he carried April, whispering down into her huge dark eyes. I held her, gently rocking the tiny bundle and praying for a miracle so that Barry could be happy again.

But there was no miracle. The teen-age love that Barry and Sally had thought so special was turning sour. Their arguments began to mingle with the dust and disarray of their apartment. It had been too much too soon.

A year slipped by — a year of anxiety for our whole family. April could not sit up unless cushioned by pillows. At first she could only smile through shining dark eyes, but it was obvious that she was bright and alert, when she began to form words without difficulty. Her sunny disposition made April a delightful child, but the medical verdict was final. April had a mild form of cerebral palsy and would never walk normally.

Barry adored his little girl, but the worry he felt for her brought a tired, haunted look to his young face. His long hours of work to care for his family were beginning to take their toll on his health. Even with help from dad, who had set them up in an apartment and given Barry a job, he could find no relief from the pressures and emotional stress that were coming from all sides. Medical bills were soaring for April's care. A mountain of problems was looming high — a mountain Barry had never intended to encounter. He was helplessly unprepared for it, and now he could climb no higher.

Suddenly Barry was home again — at first with a persisting earache, then in a haze of pain which extended to a severe headache. Soon he was in bed, tossing feverishly from side to side. An infection had crept into his mastoid and was now spreading to his brain. After nights of anguished pain, the truth surfaced and faced my parents with its awful reality.

Barry was dying. He lay in his old bedroom moaning with pain. I covered my head with my pillow, attempting to drown out the sounds of intense suffering. My brother Dan wept and pleaded with Barry to get well. Dad broke down at his bedside and had to walk away. Mother alone kept her strength and courage, sitting beside her son holding cool cloths to his feverish forehead, holding his hot hand and whispering small comforts to him.

One day he turned to her and whispered tearfully, "Please take care of April, mom. She'll need you."

By now the rift between Barry and Sally was complete. He was begging our mother to raise the little girl he knew he must leave behind. Mom nodded through brimming eyes and promised.

Early in September, Barry called dad to his bedside and in a pain-filled whisper assured him that he had "talked to the Lord and all was well." He sipped the orange juice dad held out to him and whispered, "Thanks, dad, that's enough." And he turned his face to the wall.

I slipped to his room trembling and leaned hard against the door. I knew without being told that Barry was gone. My father stood next to the bed, still holding the half-full glass of orange juice, not saying a word. My mother, sound asleep in her bedroom, would need rest for the days ahead. I turned away from that room and the awful look of death.

My dear, sweet brother who had lived for so brief a time was no more. I lay across my bed in a silent anguish, stubbornly refusing the tears that were begging to flood my face.

I was as dry-eyed at Barry's funeral, fearful that one tear would release a torrent of sobs. My oldest brother, Stephen, sat beside me as still as stone, but it was seventeen-year-old Dan who sobbed beside Barry's coffin, "I want my brother back — I want my brother back." There was no avenue of comfort for Dan — he and Barry had been inseparable friends.

I stood apart, sensing in my heart that things would never be the same for our family. I listened to the usual platitudes about "God's will" with dry eyes. *How could this be God's will?* He was supposed to be good, wasn't He? And the questions began to form again, racing through my mind without mercy. "God, why did You let this happen? It's unfair. . . unfair. . . ."

Twice now death had stood in my path — once when my playmate Ronnie had met with a violent and frightening death and now my brother whom I had adored. The "why" of it all began its relentless hammering against my brain in thundering repetitions. I could not, I would not understand.

The bitterness in my heart began to seep out into my life the day my mother, who didn't forget her promise to her son, came home carrying a two-year-old April. "Awarded by the courts to us," she smiled, and I thought grimly, "Some award."

April was a sleepless, crying child who kept my mother awake long after the morning light shone through the curtained windows. Night after sleepless night mother lay beside April on the living room floor trying to soothe her to sleep through whispers or quiet songs. It was no use. April's life was hanging by a precarious thread, her delicacy depriving her of the precious gift of sleep. I lay helpless and angry, whispering into my pillow, "O God, please let April sleep so mom can get her rest."

But instead of sleep, convulsions would often overtake April and send my parents racing to the hospital at all hours of the night. I began to watch from a greater distance with a rising resentment.

My father, helpless to effect a change in what seemed to

•

be a devastating situation, began to turn his frustration on me. I was to stay at home and help my mother. Slowly my rebellion began to find a target. Who was to blame for this topsy-turvy change of events in our lives?

Was Barry at fault? No, again it was God who had made a terrible mistake. I would never forgive Him for taking Barry and leaving April.

And so I took my first faltering step downward, unprepared for the many slippery places, crushing blows, and hurts as I struggled against the cords that were now becoming loosened. I rubbed my wrists from the soreness of being bound, stretched my body into a new freedom, and looked at the glitter around me. There was a world out there I had never dreamed existed, full of avenues of rich pleasures.

In thinking about it, the church with all its do's and don'ts was hopelessly out of date with the real world. The Bible was just a book musty with age and old ideas. I felt a flush of exhilaration as I looked about, laughing with the joy of freedom from the fear I once had of God.

Why, there had been nothing at all to fear! Why should a God who had to run a universe as vast as this care about me? I had let my childish imagination trick me, that was all. With one small backward glance, I turned and took my first step away from that safe, secure road onto the wider places.

And though my heart stirred with compassion for my mother, it was she who had made the promise to take care of April, not I. My own personal happiness and fulfillment would have to be found elsewhere.

5

Her name was Kate, and she was the new girl on the block. She had long, auburn hair and sea-green eyes that almost crinkled shut when she laughed. Kate washed my whole world with a bright new sunshine and captured my imagination with stories of places she had been and things she had seen. She was sixteen, one year older than I, and how I admired her sparkling sophisticated ways.

Escaping as often as I dared from my home, I spent more and more time with Kate. Her home was open and exciting, and there were few, if any, rules. I loved the freedom to just be myself.

We rolled back the living room rug, and Kate's young father taught me to dance. We sat at their table and played cards. Fascinated, I watched as Kate lighted a cigarette and tossed away her ashes with the flick of an experienced smoker. It wasn't long before she tapped out a cigarette for me and taught me how to inhale without choking. Soon I felt as grown up and experienced as Kate.

Kate taught me how to dress, how to wear make-up, how to talk to boys, and how to walk; and soon it became easy for me to toss back my long hair and flirt as outrageously as she.

Kate was excitement, and I was her enchanted audience. Suddenly things like piano lessons and bike rides seemed childish compared to all she had planned. She intended to go to Hollywood and become a famous movie star; and if I wanted she would send for me. I widened my eyes and nodded. Hollywood seemed like the most glamorous place in the world. We bought all the latest movie magazines and devoured the news about the thrilling lives of the stars. We lay on her living room floor and flipped the pages, sighing over the beauty of our idols, who lived in a paradise of long, glamorous gowns, cocktail parties, swimming pools, and palm trees.

We wanted to dance like Ginger Rogers, love like Maureen O'Hara, and die like Bette Davis. We saw *Dark Victory* over and over and wept each time at the bittersweet love story with such a tragic but courageous ending. We were screen-struck.

By now my life had so meshed with Kate's that I found myself agreeing wholeheartedly with her every thought. We walked arm in arm through the school halls as we entered high school — I as a freshman, Kate as a sophomore — and we began to widen our circle of friends to include a select few. First it was tall, lovely Marie, then Kate's blond Rick. One day at the malt shop we met pert Sherry, and she, too, melted into our crowd. Soon I would look up from my composition and find Tom. He completed our circle.

Tom walked me home from school on those golden autumn days. Then in October, when I was given my own car, I turned the keys over to him, and we often rode away from the busy city to the small, quiet lakes that surrounded it.

One day as we were driving aimlessly through winding tree-shaded lanes, we discovered our own "private" knoll. Sitting high above a small lake, the setting was perfect in its symmetrical beauty. The leaves were changing color, and the crisp autumn air was bringing a cooling breeze from the lake. The sun was playing hide-and-seek with the lacy white clouds that were drifting by, looking like giant pieces of cotton caught up in a vast ocean. How lovely it was that day. How happy I was to have met Tom. *If only things could stay just as they are*, I thought dreamily.

The year was drawing to a close. The thirties had been marked by the Depression and bitter hopelessness in our nation. Now perhaps with the dawning of the forties the world would find prosperity, joy, and hope. Kate Smith sang lustily "God Bless America," and we sang with her, meaning it from the bottom of our hearts.

But it was only the calm before the storm, for this would be the last year of peace our country would know for some time.

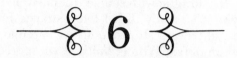

6

There is something about the end of a year that calls one to pause and reflect, almost as though now things will somehow be different and better — 1940 melting into 1941 was no exception. It was exhilarating to tune the radio into the Aragon Ballroom from nearby Chicago. When the familiar strains of "Auld Lang Syne" came floating through my room, I felt the delicious sensation that the new year was going to be wonderfully exciting.

The movie *Gone With the Wind* was playing to full theaters. Hugging my knees, I thought dreamily of Scarlett O'Hara. She was right. No matter how perplexing life could be, there would always be a tomorrow. I was determined that all my tomorrows would be shining and bright; and if once in awhile hurting memories arose in my thoughts, I, too, decided to "think about it tomorrow." The world was definitely getting better. Glenn Miller was playing the bandstands and recording his "certain sound." The Big Band Era was in.

The previous November Wendell Wilke had determined to get Roosevelt out of office. Why was everyone I knew so upset with Roosevelt, the only president I could remember? Personally I liked President Roosevelt and more so when I discovered that Kate's folks were voting for him. That settled it for me.

The radio and newspapers were warning that Paris would soon fall to the Nazis. England was under heavy bombing. But none of this news struck any terror to our hearts. England and France were worlds away.

Besides, my world during the fall of 1940 had been football games and parties and dances on Saturday nights.

One night when we were jammed into a booth at the malt shop, the air blue with smoke, Johnny walked into our lives. Maybe it was silly, but I felt a strange premonition about him right away. He wove his way around the tables and leaned on ours. "Who is *that?*" I whispered to Tom.

"A new guy, a senior," Tom said, and his eyes narrowed. I knew right away that Tom didn't like him. Johnny was dressed in the "zoot suit" that had just come into fashion, and he whistled through his teeth, which was enough to make me dislike him right there. His dark hair was slicked back, and he looked like a character out of a James Cagney movie. His eyes skimmed over our crowd and rested on Sherry.

"Let's dance." It was a command, and Sherry jumped up. From that night on they were a twosome. We allowed Johnny into our crowd just because Sherry was our friend. But he let Marie, Kate, and I know from the beginning that Sherry was his exclusive property.

One night sitting around the pavilion at Green Lake the guys began another discussion of the real possibility that America might enter the war. Tom was sure he would join the navy, because he loved the sea; Rick thought about the adventure of faraway places; but Johnny just laughed. He was sitting, his feet propped up on the rail, smoking a cigarette, and staring off into the black waters.

"I don't believe in war," he shrugged. "Like I said, we shouldn't get into it. It's every man for himself, and we shouldn't be poking around in Hitler's business. Draft or no draft, I won't be fighting in any war." He flicked the stub of his cigarette into the lake and stood up. Sherry joined him quickly, and they walked off into the darkness, their arms wrapped about each other's waists.

"I don't like that guy," Tom said staring after them. "There's just something about him I don't like." His voice trailed off. I agreed. Johnny was a mystery to all of us. I couldn't understand how the buoyant, vibrant Sherry could stand his dark, brooding ways. But now even Sherry had changed. The cheerful, animated smile was gone, and she seemed quiet and strained.

One day Johnny disappeared. He simply vanished from sight. When we called Sherry, she was cold and distant. Finally we discovered the truth. Marie called me one day in late September and whispered on the phone as if she were afraid of being heard.

"Sherry's pregnant."

I hadn't seen Sherry since school started, but someone said she had the flu, and I had been too busy getting into the new semester to wonder any more about it. I turned to watch my mother working in the kitchen and lowered my voice.

"How do you know?"

Marie talked swiftly. "Her mother told me. Johnny's nowhere to be found." Marie sounded so desolate I could hardly speak.

I murmured something about calling Kate and wondered if we should try to see Sherry.

"There's nothing we can do," Marie said flatly. "Her mother won't even let her friends near her."

By October the whole school knew, and everyone spoke in cloistered whispers, some of them sniffing, "That's good enough for her messing around with that greasy character."

Suddenly there was more bad news — a word that filled us with cold dread.

Abortion.

"Sherry's had an abortion." Marie was close to tears as we met in the hall. She said that Sherry had been taken to the other side of town, and in some dark, dirty room, her baby was taken from her young body. When something went wrong, she had been rushed by ambulance to a downtown hospital.

Later that day Marie and I sat with Kate in her backyard and talked about our young friend in hushed whispers. I remember now the crispness of that fall day, and the smell of burning leaves still brings Sherry to mind. It was cold, and soon the snow would fall. I remembered Sherry ice-skating, whirling around gracefully, smiling and singing among the swirling snowflakes. It seemed impossible that she now lay close to death. I burst into sobs, and Kate and Marie joined me.

As soon as we were allowed to see her, Marie and I drove to the hospital. Silent and somber, we let the elevator take us to the fourth floor. What could we say to Sherry?

There she was — just as though nothing had happened. Her curly blond hair framed her round face; her blue eyes sparkled. She sat up in bed looking fragile, like a pink-and-white flower. She never mentioned Johnny nor the horrors of what had happened to her.

Her record player was at her bedside, and she was singing along to the latest tunes. We began to relax, laughing and talking about school and who was dating whom. It didn't seem as if we were in a small white room at all but out at the lake just like old times.

I have often wondered what Sherry must have been feeling that day as she chatted with us about ordinary things. Did she wonder about the baby she would never see? Did she lie awake at night fighting off the nightmare of pain and a screaming ambulance and doctors' worried faces and the hushed whispers of her family around her bed? Did she still love Johnny? Or did she want to be rid of his memory forever? We never knew. If her heart ached, she didn't let it show. She seemed cheerful and happy, just like her old self.

For one brief moment I felt uneasy in that stark, colorless room. Sherry might have died, and it was I who knew all the Bible verses about life and death — the memories that couldn't be forgotten. I knew what the Bible said about the way to eternal life, and I had never told Sherry. Indeed how could I when I myself thought so little about it? Still, I felt certain in my heart that all I had learned as a child was unmistakably true: Eternal life was given only to those who accepted God's gift of Himself with an open and repentant heart. My throat closed. I was glad she hadn't died.

Sherry saw the tears in my eyes and said cheerfully, "Don't cry." She lifted her blanket and sat up in bed. "Well, I wanted to lose weight, and now I'll have the best figure in town." Marie and I looked away. We couldn't believe how thin she had become.

Just then a nurse walked in, giving us meaningful glances to indicate that it was time to go. Marie and I stood up.

"Hey, kids, don't go," Sherry pleaded, and we turned at the door. Marie walked back and held Sherry's hand for just a moment. I smiled my good-by. How often I have wished that we had stayed at Sherry's pleading, for it was the last time Marie and I saw our dear friend alive.

Sherry died quietly the following Friday when her lungs began to fill. She never saw or talked to Johnny. Her mother's arms were holding her close under the oxygen tent as she drew her last breath.

Two days before Sherry died, my mother had asked our pastor to visit her, and I sighed, "Oh, mom, how come?" But secretly I was glad. If I couldn't tell Sherry about God, maybe our pastor could. He did. He sat by her bedside, speaking words of comfort and assurance from God's Word while she struggled to breathe. Then he asked if she believed, Sherry turned to smile and nod, her blue eyes glistening with tears.

She was buried on a cold, wet November afternoon. Rick, Bob, and Tom were three of the pallbearers, but Johnny was conspicuously absent. Marie, Kate, and I walked beside the casket in silent sorrow.

I thought I saw Johnny across the street slumped over behind a tree, just staring and smoking. I never did know if it was he, and no one ever heard from him again.

Marie and I visited Sherry's mother often and sat in her

parlor, listening to her while she rocked slowly back and forth and talked about her daughter. Pictures of Sherry were everywhere about the house, and one day we discovered a recording that Sherry had made of herself singing "All or Nothing at All." We all wept together, remembering. Sherry was gone forever from our lives, and all we had to remind us were warm, vibrant memories, laughing pictures, and a husky voice on a scratchy recording.

7

November faded into an overcast December. It was to be a memorable December, for on the seventh day in a surprise attack, the Japanese bombed our naval base in a place called Pearl Harbor.

In his familiar drawl, our president declared America to be at war. Our family, like others across the nation, sat around the radio in stunned belief. Where or what was Pearl Harbor? And hadn't the Japanese just signed a peace treaty with us?

The Christmas holidays lost their magic that year, for soon boys were standing in line at the recruiting stations, impatient to get into uniform. Everyday someone else dropped out of school to enter some branch of the service. Rick was first from our crowd, lightheartedly saying good-by at the train station with adventure and excitement in his eyes.

Kate dropped out of school almost immediately, her sophistication carrying her beyond the world of teen-agers. She got a job singing in a small nightclub on the west side of town.

But my deepest fear was surfacing more each day. Tom was becoming more silent and withdrawn; and finally on New Year's Eve, his words falling over each other, he told me, "I'm enlisting, right after the holidays. I'll miss you,

Maggie." I knew he was trying to ease the hurt by using his teasing nickname for me. "Here, I want you to have this." He tugged at his class ring, and I clutched it, closing my fist over its warm hardness.

"I'll wait for you, Tom," I managed to say, still holding his ring.

We talked for hours sitting in my convertible while the snow beat mercilessly on the top, like an ominous drum warning that Tom was going . . . going . . . going. . . .

In February, on a bitterly cold morning, I stood with Tom in the railway station holding tightly to his hand. I cried, my face hidden in his shoulder, while he held me gently.

Finally Tom took my face in his hands and spoke intensely, "We both got off to a wrong start in school, and it's too late for me. But do you remember the promise you made me that day at the lake? Will you promise that you'll graduate even if it means changing schools?"

I couldn't answer because my throat was choked with a lump, so he put his finger under my chin and said it again, "Promise?"

"I promise, Tom," I said, but I was still crying.

Suddenly he brightened. "Hey, I'll be back, you know. I have a leave in thirty days."

And through my quiet sobbing I nodded, but I wondered grimly if my old enemy death was about to snatch another person away from me, a person I deeply cared about. I watched the train chug slowly out of the station, car after car of blurred faces pressed to windows — smiling, weeping, waving, a generation of young men were saying good-by to a life that would never be the same. Through my tear-filled eyes, I saw Tom in every face. I wondered if I would ever see him again.

I didn't. Somewhere in the Pacific, after a canceled leave in the early spring of 1941, a navy ship went down in the night. My sweet Tom was on that ship, and he went to the bottom of that deep blue ocean.

My heart went down with him for a very long time.

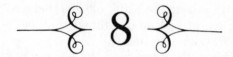

8

I had to get out of the house. I had been living in a misty haze until the truth finally penetrated — Tom was nowhere in the world. There was no one to talk to, no one who could understand the hurting loss of even the smallest memories.

One night when my parents were asleep, I wrote a short note, threw some clothes in a bag, and tiptoed cautiously down the winding staircase. Backing my car out as quietly as possible, I drove aimlessly until weariness finally forced me to stop. I curled up in the front seat and slept fitfully until the morning sun awakened me.

It was no use. I couldn't stand the thought of being alone. Even the stillness in the car seemed unbearable, and so I found Patty, a girl I knew only slightly, and she called her friend Dotty, and we were off, giggling nervously at the prospect of a new adventure. Without gas stamps, we had no choice except to park my Plymouth on the edge of town. We stood, our thumbs held up for a ride to anywhere at all.

Once we stopped at a roadside cafe and met a small, forlorn girl who told us her name was Marianne. She wanted to tag alone, and we shrugged, not really caring.

The heavy humidity in the air finally turned to a drenching rain. We stood in the downpour, our long hair stringy and sodden, thumbs begging for a ride from passing cars. We wanted anyone to stop, anyone at all.

Finally someone did stop — a black-and-white police car. Marianne turned pale, and we fell into an uncomfortable silence on the ride to the police station. I shifted my gaze and examined the ceiling while the police officer lectured on the evils of hitchhiking. Our desolate new friend was really a chronic runaway from a girls' institution, and when they led her away, we stared after her with pity and disbelief.

After promising the police officers that we would take a bus home, we picked up our things quite self-consciously and left with pounding hearts.

My Plymouth, waiting on the narrow road where we had parked it, was the most welcome sight in the world. I wanted to be home in my pink-and-white bedroom with its gingham bedspread and ruffled curtains filtering the bright sunshine. The thought of taking a bath and sleeping forever was foremost in my mind, even diminishing my fear of what my parents would say.

My father furiously tightened his lips and for once in his life didn't know what to say. My mother tearfully held out her arms. They knew nothing of Tom. I shared none of my outside life with them. How could they know the emptiness I felt since his death or share my grief? They thought my sadness was simply rebellion.

But the weekend escapade had fully convinced me that the emptiness within could not be left behind by running away — it would follow me wherever I went. I had lost Tom. Forever! There was no turning back to the time of those carefree days when we had smiled into each other's eyes and shared a young tenderness which had seemed so complete. It was all over. Tom was dead. Alone in my room I said the words aloud so I could believe they were true.

Thinking sadly of the emptiness of life, I brushed my long hair over and over, letting the tears flow down my cheeks and splash on my mirrored dressing table. "Tom is dead. Tom is dead." I repeated the words, forcing my mind to comprehend what my heart could not.

It was the war that had turned my world upside down. Yes, that was it. As soon as the war was over and everything was back to normal, I'd find that elusive something to fill the aching void that cried out for inner satisfaction.

I couldn't think about it any more tonight. I was exhausted. But sometime soon my world would be set in order again. I switched on my bedside radio and half smiled as I listened to the lovely song, "When the Lights Go On Again All Over the World." Of course, that was it. The lights had gone out for a short time, but soon they would flood on with a new brilliance and bring back lost joys.

My thoughts mingled with the words of the song of hope for a better world until the soft background music could no longer be heard.

I slept soundly without dreaming.

9

How is it possible to walk through school corridors swarming with chattering, shouting students and feel so isolated? In a reverie of daydreams I'd stroll absent-mindedly, absorbed in past memories. Often I'd think that maybe around the next corner I'd bump into Tom, he'd reach for my books, and we'd whisper, "What a nice day for a ride," scamper out the back door, into my car, and across town to the lake. But Tom wouldn't be around any corner ever again. My loneliness deepened each day.

One day while reminiscing, I recalled something Tom had said to me. We had been parked on our own "private hill" overlooking Reeds Lake. The day had been exceptionally beautiful. The outline of the shores etched so clearly on the horizon was like a magnificent painting.

"You know, I think about God a lot." Tom turned to me as though I should understand this thought. "I mean just look at that sparkling lake and blue sky and beautiful white clouds." He waved his hand, gesturing over the gorgeous landscape. "Look at the trees, hundreds of years old and still so majestic. There *must* be a God, don't you think?"

As usual, at the mention of that Name I stirred uneasily. I smiled and murmured something about the possibility of a divine Presence who had created all of this beauty — and changed the subject. What could *I* tell Tom about God? There seemed to be nothing to say.

The poignant memory of that day and Tom's searching question drove me deeper and deeper into despair.

Marie decided to transfer to a downtown Catholic high school, and then I was even more forlorn in my misty solitude.

There were memories everywhere. Driving home from school past the ice-cream parlor and remembering our after-school dances brought a sharp pang of grief. Once my blue convertible found its way to our own little hill, and the car radio complied with my mood by softly playing, "I'll Never Smile Again."

I didn't think I ever would.

One night I felt a longing for the past, so I went to the nightclub where Kate was singing. She was as sparkling as ever, captivating the servicemen who crowded around her. Kate had lost none of her magic.

She sat at my table and ordered two drinks; I sipped mine distastefully. Our voices were lost in the din of the blaring music and loud laughter. The longer Kate sat at my table flirting openly with any serviceman who caught her eye, the more I wondered why I had ever thought her someone to admire and follow.

A curly haired sailor leaned across the table and asked me to dance, but I could only stare at him until he became uncomfortable. I had never seen Tom in his uniform except in a blurred snapshot taken on the deck of a ship. "O God," I thought, "why have I had to face death so often?"

"All alone and lonely," the jukebox wailed, and I left the table and stumbled out the door, across the graveled parking lot, and into my car. I lay my head on the steering wheel and burst into bitter tears.

As I wept, there was an underlying cry, "O God in heaven, if You *are* there, help me. O God. . . ." Over and over I sobbed His name until the tears flooded my face. I could hardly see the road as I drove home. The darkness of the night seemed like daylight compared to the gloom overwhelming my spirit.

The thought began to spin around in my mind, "Life isn't worth living any more." Gradually, like an orchestra tuning its instruments for a great symphony, the words became a mounting crescendo thundering in my head, "Life isn't worth living any more. Life isn't worth living any more."

I lay on my bed fully dressed, thinking that the sweet peace of death would come as a welcome friend. I remembered Anne, a girl I had known in junior high school, who had swallowed a whole bottle of her mother's sleeping pills, ending her life. *What could have been so terrible for her to do such a thing?* I had wondered in horror. Now I understood. Life had become a towering mountain too high for Anne to climb.

As I lay in anguish, another thought locked me in a cold grip surpassing the wish to die. *What if God really is on the other side?* I curled into a miserable ball and sobbed quietly. I was tired of life, afraid of life. But I was more afraid of death. I was afraid, so afraid. The thought of facing the valley of the shadow of death immobilized me. And so I fell into a troubled, restless sleep. But in the inner recesses of my mind a refrain was still struggling to be heard. "O God, O God, *O God!*"

10

Every day the lines were longer at the recruiting stations, and each week more names were added to the missing or killed-in-action list. The war was becoming more personal and increasingly tragic as the names of my friends and classmates began to appear.

Our favorite band leaders were laying down their batons and getting into uniform. The latest hit songs began to reflect the atmosphere of a full-scale war.

We were singing "This Is the Army, Mr. Jones" or more tearfully, "The White Cliffs of Dover." Movies were telling sad, pain-filled stories of the tragedy of war and lost loves. The faces of familiar movie stars were disappearing from the screen.

But as for me, it seemed that the war was already over and lost when Tom was killed. I wrote regularly to the guys who begged for mail, trying to write cheery letters to boost their morale, but mine was suffering so badly that it was a real effort.

Our town became a base for a Naval Air Cadet School. A few of us high school girls would sip Cokes with them at the drugstore after school, exchanging names and addresses and every so often accepting an invitation to a dance at their base.

I thought of the old saying, "Time heals all wounds,"

and I wondered bitterly "How *much* time?" When I heard one of "our songs" on the radio, saw a curly haired sailor, or turned a certain corner, Tom was in my heart again.

At last summer arrived and brought with it a sense of relief. School had become the most painful reminder of things I wanted to forget. Day after day I lay listlessly on our porch swing leafing through magazines or listening to radio serials until I'd doze off to sleep.

Little April was on miniature crutches now. I felt a stir of pity for this little dark-haired girl who had a way of smiling at me out of Barry's shining eyes. She would never know the joy of racing through windswept clover fields or of climbing huge twisted oak trees or of swimming far out into the lake and floating back on small waves.

My mother was a quiet wonder. She remained steady and sweet through long days and nights of caring for April. She had a promise to keep, but it had gone far beyond duty into genuine love. Barry's little girl had become her own.

July brought with it an unusual simmering heat, and when Kate surprised me with a telephone call and asked if I'd like to join her and her parents at a cottage for a week, it sounded like fun. We would swim and lie on the little beach, Kate promised; so excitedly we made plans.

At first it seemed like old times. We spent rainy evenings playing cards with Kate's parents or dancing to their radio in the little cottage. Sunning ourselves on the sandy beach, we reminisced about the gang. We smoked endlessly, rowing far out onto the grassy lake, letting the little rowboat drift us back to shore.

I was unprepared and stunned when Kate finally blurted out that she was pregnant by one of the guys in the band. He didn't want to get married, and she didn't know what to do. She hadn't told her parents yet. She hid her face in her hands and my heart sank.

Thinking of Sherry, I cried out: "Kate, how could you do it?"

Kate's face appeared more tender than I had ever seen it when she whispered, "I thought he loved me."

The rest of the week I just listened to Kate as she poured out her misery, and though for years I had resented my many restrictions, for once I was glad. For one short moment, I even felt gratitude for my parents.

When the week was over, we rode home from the lake a bit more subdued. Her parents thought we were tired, and we were. Kate was weary from the weight of her unshared burden, and I was tired of the endless search for permanent happiness. I had begged Kate not to do anything foolish as Sherry had, and she had nodded miserably. They left me at my door, and I turned and waved at Kate's partially hidden face in the back seat.

Kate and her parents moved out of town soon after, and only once did I talk to Kate again — years later as she was passing through town, changing trains on her way to a new job singing in a nightclub in the South. Our conversation competed with the clamor of the railway station. She wondered about me and had just a moment to say hello. We promised to keep in touch.

But we never did. Kate is a poignant memory and a bittersweet reminder of the way things were.

11

"Mom," I asked one December day, "if there is a God, why did He allow April to be born crippled? It's not fair, you know." It was impossible to keep the bitterness out of my voice.

Mother was washing clothes in the basement, and the Monday morning smell of soap and starch filled the room. I sat down on the stairs to watch her. Even pinning clothes to the line she had a lovely grace and beauty.

I expected to hear a lecture on the virtues of trusting God no matter what happened, but she was silent for so long that I thought she wasn't going to answer at all. Finally she slipped a clothespin from her mouth and said quietly, "The picture isn't finished yet."

"What is that supposed to mean? April didn't ask to be born."

"It all seems confusing now, like a painting that has just been started. Often the picture makes no sense at all, but a true artist knows what the finished product will be. It's already completed in his mind. He knows he will have a magnificent work of art."

"How do you know that?" I was angry, because, aside from April, I was thinking about Tom and Sherry and about the thousands of boys who returned from the war wounded or those who wouldn't come back at all. I didn't mention these thoughts but pursued the question of April. "Aren't you tired of taking care of April? Aren't you the least bit mad at God for letting Barry die?"

My mother stopped, and when she looked at me, her blue eyes were brimming with tears. I felt a little cruel, but to me it seemed so unfair. I simply couldn't understand her unshaken faith in a God who would permit such injustice.

"Honey," she said, "if I didn't believe God and know that He is working to make the final picture perfect, then, yes, I *would* be angry. Sometimes I grieve deeply over losing your brother, and I hurt so for little April. But when you are passing through a trial the Lord goes through it with you. And ultimately, honey, God causes all things to work together for good. And when the picture is finished there is great joy."

"I want some of that joy *now*."

"There *is* joy now," she smiled, knowing that I couldn't understand. "It comes from trusting God. Abiding in Christ — walking with Him — brings joy. And you'll see someday that there is no lasting joy anywhere else."

"Barry was too young to die," I said abruptly. And Tom, too, my heart cried.

"I know — ," Mom paused, her eyes beginning to fill with tears again. "But you know Barry has God's *best* now. He's with the Lord, which is far better. Someday — someday perhaps you will understand a mother's heart. Of course there will always be a longing for Barry, and we'll always miss him. He was so happy —, remember how we called him 'sunshine'?" And she smiled remembering.

I jumped up quickly and ran upstairs, away from the tears I knew would flow. I was only seventeen. I was too young to have faced death so often. I wanted to live life to its fullest now.

But I couldn't know that cold December morning, when my whole life was in revolt over unanswered questions, that it *was* possible for grief to mingle with joy.

If God was truly painting my picture, then He certainly was using all drab colors. When I longed so much for brightness, light, and finished beauty, everything seemed gray, dark, and incomplete.

February and the new semester would be here soon. A cold shiver ran through me with the thought of walking once more through the halls of Southeast High. There seemed to be no place to hide from pain-filled memories.

It's a funny thing about memories. The ones you want to remember seem shadowy, mysteriously dimmed by the passing of time. But the remembrances you would rather forget surface over and over again, haunting your mind.

It was my father who solved the problem for me. It was late December, and I was sitting on the sofa watching the snow fall softly against the windowpane when he turned from his desk to answer the question that lay silently in my thoughts.

"How would you like to transfer to another school?" He watched my startled face and continued, "If you would, I'll pay the tuition. If it would make you any happier, that is."

Tom's last words flooded my mind, and I could hardly answer. I told my father I didn't know where I would go, but, yes, that was what I wanted to do. He turned back to the desk and sighed heavily.

Regretfully, I wished that somehow I could please him. If I could transfer away from past memories and find new surroundings and new friends, I would turn over a new leaf, I vowed to myself. Pity stirred within me, for I loved my dad, and I knew he loved me though we had a difficult time communicating that love.

When he spoke, his voice was heavy. "You find a school, and you can start in February. I'd like to see you away from that crowd."

What he didn't know was "that crowd" had already disintegrated and I was alone. I kissed him on the cheek, and as always when I displayed the smallest bit of affection, he melted.

"Thanks, dad, that's what I really want to do."

He didn't look up from his papers but said quietly, "It's not *the* answer, you know, but it is an answer for now."

"Dad," I turned around at the dining room door. "Just because I'm going to change schools doesn't mean I want to be a Christian. Don't set your heart on that. I could never go that route. I have to be free, free to think for myself. I don't want anyone else's ideas forced on me."

He didn't look up, so I continued, "I just want you to know, that's all."

I felt a new excitement stirring within me as I thought of starting life all over again. New friends and new places would cover the wounds of the past years. I could never be a goody-goody like the girls at church, but maybe I'd stop smoking, staying out so late, hanging around the night spots.

I imagined myself in a new school, making new friends, getting good grades, and pleasing my parents. With those thoughts, a feeling of relief swept over me. I could do it. I could do it on my own, without religion, without God, and without the church. It was simply a matter of will-power. ·

That night, lying in bed, I smiled in the dark, switched off my radio, and fell into a sleep that brought with it a recurring dream. I dreamt I was running through a meadow with Tom, but he was far ahead of me. I was calling and calling for him, but when I finally reached him and held him to me, it wasn't Tom at all. A sob caught at my throat and I awoke.

I knew I wouldn't find Tom again, but just as certainly I knew that someday I would be satisfied, fulfilled, and find true meaning to my life. Someday, somewhere, my dreams would come true.

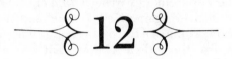

The January snow made our town a winter wonderland, and driving had become hazardous. It was a Saturday afternoon, and I thought the brisk, cold air might clear my mind, so I backed my Plymouth out of our snow-covered driveway onto the plowed street.

I turned on the car radio and hummed along with a new tune recorded by Tommy Dorsey, "I Dream of You." My heart was agreeing that my dreams were still of Tom and the sweet romance we had shared.

I stopped for a red light and drummed my fingers on the steering wheel — the same wheel that Tom had hugged so tightly when he had told me he was joining the navy. It seemed a lifetime ago. I glanced to my left and noticed two small boys working on an almost-completed snowman. I smiled, remembering happier, younger days when I had thought playing in the snow the most exciting thing in the world. The boys' hands were encased in mittens frozen to their fingers, crusted with tiny cakes of snow. They looked so cold, and I wondered if there would be a wide floor heater to warm them and maybe some hot chocolate waiting as there had always been for me.

Suddenly I realized that I was looking directly at a

school playground, and just beyond the boys was a brown brick building almost hidden behind a clump of barren trees. Now in the January sunshine the school became plainly visible. Across the top was the name of a high school I had never seen before.

The light turned green. I made a left turn and stopped. Something told me that I was supposed to be here on this particular Saturday afternoon and that here was the high school I would attend. Small and new, even in the freezing winds, it looked warm and inviting. I stared for a long time before my gloved hand caught the door handle and pulled it open. I stumbled across the street, my saddle shoes filled with snow, walked the short distance to the entrance, and pushed open the heavy double doors.

The halls were empty. I had never been in a school on a Saturday afternoon before, and it filled me with a strange feeling. The lockers stood in silent rows in a sort of hushed expectancy awaiting the new term. To my left was a winding staircase. It was a short distance to the second floor, and walking slowly up the stairs, I scarcely felt the wetness of my saddle shoes or the biting cold of my hands.

A janitor was sweeping the already-clean floors and looked at me as if to question my presence. But I had already spotted the office marked "Principal," and seeing the door ajar, I knocked and waited.

I heard a soft "Come in," and then I was standing before the lovely Mrs. Walker, elegantly beautiful with a warmth that radiated through her blue eyes. She looked at me questioningly, and I cleared my throat, trying to find the right words.

"May I help you?" She indicated for me to sit down.

"I was just driving by and saw your school." It sounded so ridiculous I wanted to start over.

"Yes?"

"And I was wondering — well, I'd like to come here. I'll be in the last half of my junior year next month. I'd just like to finish here."

"Do you have friends here at Oakdale?" She furrowed her brow, and I shifted uncomfortably.

"No, I don't. I don't know anybody here."

"Then — why? Why do you want to come here?"

How could I explain to this lovely soft-spoken woman that I needed a change, that I could no longer live with my memories, that I wanted my life to be different, that I was going to be a new person and needed new surroundings? I kept searching for the right words, but they wouldn't come.

"I don't know," I said. "I'd just like to come to a smaller school."

She shifted some papers on her desk and was thoughtful for a moment. Then almost as if she surprised herself, she spoke in a puzzled tone.

"It would cost tuition, of course, because you are out of our district."

"I know — my father will pay."

"What is your name?" she asked suddenly, perhaps wanting to label this seventeen-year-old girl who had walked in unannounced with such an unusual request. I told her, and she wrote it down. Then she handed me a sheaf of papers.

"Well, I've no idea why you want to come to our school, but have your father sign these papers. You may start the new semester in February."

I took the papers and folded them carefully. She couldn't know what her decision would mean to me, nor could I at that moment.

"Thank you, Mrs. Walker. I'll be here in February. I'll look forward to attending this school, and I'll do my best to fulfill your trust in me."

I meant it at the time. I felt that I could really make my own dreams come true. With a little self-confidence, fortitude, charm, and a little money — I smiled, patting the papers — dreams really could come true.

My father signed the tuition papers and enclosed a sizeable check for the first semester. I thought happily how easy it was to change one's direction. In just one month I would embark on a new adventure in life, and I was positive it would hold all the fulfillment I longed for. I was the winner after all.

That night I smiled smugly as I climbed into bed. I was about to find that intangible happiness that had so long eluded me; and if in my deepest thoughts there was the smallest doubt, I pushed it from my conscious mind and let the warmth of my present happiness lull me into a deep, untroubled sleep.

— ⚜ 13 ⚜ —

The world looked infinitely better that cold February morning as I began to dress for my first day at Oakdale High School. I deliberated a long time at my closet, and I changed my outfit three times before I finally decided on a white pleated skirt and pink angora sweater. I brushed my hair until it shone. The excitement and apprehension of beginning all over, of meeting new friends, made it impossible for me to eat the breakfast my mother had lovingly prepared.

Butterflies were chasing themselves round and round in my stomach, and I almost wondered why l had started the whole thing. But the transfer papers were signed, and there was no backing out. With a wildly beating heart, I began the short walk to the bus stop, leaving my car in the driveway to save gas coupons. When the huge bus came into view through the gray morning mist, I nearly turned and ran the short block back home.

But I didn't. I got on the bus and chose a seat next to a pert brunette. She greeted me warmly and said her name was Laurie. This was her third year at Oakdale High, though she now lived outside the district with her aunt, following her mother's death. Before we arrived at the school, Laurie and I were laughing together like old friends.

It was easy to see that Laurie was one of the most popular girls in the school. She had the unique quality of accepting each person as he was. Laurie was sought after by the boys and was voted the "prettiest girl in school" each year. Her chestnut hair framed her pretty heart-shaped face, and she walked with a slight limp, which added to her charm. She introduced me to everyone we met and I felt lucky to meet such a vivacious girl the first day. We shared lockers and she walked me to my classes. For the first time in almost two years, I found myself able to forget the past and enjoy the present.

The smallness of Oakdale made our class close-knit, like a family. The teachers were scarcely older than the students and were excited about the new methods of progressive education, with the emphasis on social activities. For me school became a country club, and my spirits began to soar. The "Coffee Cup" was jammed with kids during lunch hours and after school. The jukebox blared out the latest tunes, enveloping me in a world I knew.

It was true. All I had needed was a change of atmosphere and a new group of friends. I could be my happy self again.

When the late March sun melted the snow, transforming it into mush, spring began to blossom. Now I was able to drive to school for the last two months of the semester. I had just met Janie, and we talked about warm afternoons at the lake. To Laurie's obvious displeasure, I was caught up with Janie's crowd.

"We're having a party Saturday night," Janie whispered one day in class. "The cadets from the navy school will be there, and we'll have plenty to drink." Her eyes were twinkling with excitement, and I nodded my assent.

Casually I told Laurie about Janie's party, but she frowned. "I hope you don't go — her parties get pretty wild."

"I can handle myself," I retorted. I felt ready for some of the old excitement. Thinking it over, I decided it wouldn't be fair to judge Janie until I went to one of her parties and saw for myself what they were like.

The radio was already blaring when I arrived, and the living room was full of young people from Oakdale and the navy school. Most of them were opening cans of beer and whiskey bottles. The room was thick with smoke, and I was beginning to feel a little uneasy when Janie shouted a greeting. Suddenly it was like the old days with the gang.

I let one of the cadets light my cigarette and felt a new surge of confidence. Drinking just enough to make me silly, I danced, whirling around the floor. Soon the faces blurred into one.

Sometimes I would close my eyes and imagine I was dancing with Tom, and then I would lay my cheek against an unfamiliar face and hum along to "Let's get lost, lost in another world."

That was exactly what I wanted to do. To get lost forever. Lost from hurting memories. Lost from my parent's religion and disapproval. Lost from the strain of watching April struggle on her crutches. I felt giddy wishing I could be lost in another world. But in the deepest part of my heart I knew that I was already lost and couldn't find myself. I felt fragmented and shattered, truly lost to all that I wished to be.

I was nearly the last one to leave the party. I drove home slowly; the cool breeze was refreshing and would hopefully diminish the smell of smoke and alcohol that had saturated my clothes.

I tiptoed upstairs and undressed quietly. It was a game I played to see how late I could come in and how quietly I could maneuver in the dark and slip into bed without awakening my parents.

Sitting on the edge of my bed, I recalled what a fun party it had been — and yet, why wasn't I happy? Why, for instance, did I feel like washing my entire body until I could be clean from the smoke that was clinging to my clothes and hair? Why did I want to shut out the thought of the vulgar language that fell from lips that were loose with alcohol?

Why did I feel empty and forlorn as I tasted the bitterness of ashes in my mouth?

I pulled the blanket over my head and wept softly. Nothing had changed. The new leaf that I had so carefully turned over was already besmirched, and something told me that every time I turned over another new page it would end up smudged and dirty again. I was the same person, only in different surroundings.

I fell asleep on a tear-stained pillow and awoke late the next afternoon with a pounding headache. Soon the semester would be over, and though I had loved Oakdale High, it hadn't brought me the happiness I had longed for.

On Monday morning I tried to avoid Laurie in civics class, but she was not so easily put off. She gave my foot a little kick and asked, "How was Janie's party?"

I shrugged, "It wasn't so bad."

"Why do you want to mess up your life?" she persisted.

I laughed and was immediately sorry, for the laugh was hollow and high-pitched. "Just by going to Janie's party? Oh, come on — ." I wanted the best of both worlds. I liked the popularity of being Laurie's best friend, but I also had the old urge for complete freedom from rules and regulations. Conventional lines were meant to be crossed. I hated rules! Who made them anyway? Who had a right to tell anyone else what they could or could not do?

The days of April and May were glorious as the trees began to blossom and almost hide our small brick school from view. I parked my car outside homeroom, and when the temptation was too great, Janie and friends would hop in and off we'd go, heading for the small lakes fringing our town.

The heat of the city far behind, we relished the cool breezes under the giant oak trees. We swam far out to the huge floating raft and lay motionless on its large wooden planks. The water, cool and still, was a lulling contrast to the blazing sun beating down on our faces.

I could lie on the softly rocking raft, watch the rippling waves, and find a small measure of peace. I tried hard not to think of how unfair it had been for me to lose the only person I cared for in a war that seemed eternal. I desperately strived to forget Sherry's laughing face as I remembered her popping in and out of the water. How terrible for anyone to have to die at the young age of sixteen. She had just begun to live, and suddenly she was gone.

That would never happen to me. If there was any joy in my cup, I would drink it now before something dreadful happened again. No one knew what tomorrow would bring, so as long as I was alive, I would make the most of it. I was having plenty of fun now. I was really living, wasn't I? Well — wasn't I?

14

Our class voted to have its junior-senior picnic at Green Lake that year, and memories hit me hard as my car swung down the familiar dirt road facing the lake. I hadn't been back since the last night Tom and I had danced together on the deck.

Everything was just the same. How could the pavilion just stand there as though nothing had changed? There was the same wooden deck; rowboats, looking as though they hadn't moved one bit, still bobbed up and down in the waters; and the same green picnic tables huddled under the giant oak trees. I felt affronted at the sameness of it all.

Laurie and I lay on the beach shading our eyes from the sun which was blazing down on the hot sand. Finally she spoke: "You're awfully quiet today. Anything wrong?"

I didn't answer for a moment. I was busy watching the kids chasing each other into the water. Some members of the class were dancing and others were sitting, legs dangling over the rail, munching on candy bars. I fought back the bitter tears which were lying just under the surface.

Life was unbearably sad, and it was the war that had started it all.

"Laurie — " I really wanted to know — "are you happy?"

She broke into a grin. "Let's put it this way — if happy is

breathing and eating, then I'm happy. What else is there?"

Laurie was right. There wasn't anything else, and I was about to say so when she jumped to her feet to join the kids splashing in the water.

I had often wanted to tell her about Tom, but the words stuck in my throat. I wanted her to know about Sherry and how she had loved too much and settled for too little. Again words refused to form sentences. It seemed important to me to make Laurie understand why I went to Janie's parties, but when I tried to explain it didn't make any sense.

I rolled over on the sand and hid my head in my arms. I was talking to *God* again, and try as I would to stop, my thoughts were pleading with Him to understand, to filter out my confusion, to make some sense out of my broken life. In spite of all the noise around me, I fell asleep on the warm, comforting sand.

Abruptly I was awakened to the tugging and pulling of four boys and thrown into the icy waters of Green Lake, surfacing wet and choking. The dip into the water lightened my spirits, and I ate my picnic lunch in a better mood.

The ride home was filled with talk of the lucky seniors who would soon be saying good-by to the halls of Oakdale. Boys were already signing up for various branches of the service and girls were talking of joining the WAVES or WACS. We juniors groaned about having to face one more year.

My senior year was going to be a good one, I decided that night as I washed the sand from my hair, setting it in tiny pin curls. This time I resolved that I would muster all my will-power, pull good grades, and stay away from Janie's parties.

For once I was right. When the next big wave carried me high on its crest, I would helplessly let go of the stern once and for all.

Sunday morning came much too early. It was the end of June, and summer was radiating warm sunshine even in the early morning hours. I rolled over in bed, tired from the night before when "just one more time" I had gone to a cadet party with Janie on the outskirts of town. Falling into bed, exhausted after staying out much later than usual and knowing that to appease my parents I would have to be up early for church, I tossed and turned, begging for sleep.

Pressing my head against the coolness of the car window during the ride to church, I dozed, aware that my parents sadly disapproved of my late hours the night before. April, sitting next to me, felt the tension and remained silent.

The hymns were sung without me; the announcements missed my attention. I sat apart, folding my arms to ward off any attempts at friendly conversation. I wondered what these "church kids" did for fun. Did they really *believe* in their own pious words *faith* and *trust?*

Remembering back many years before when our Sunday school teacher Uncle Paul had lost his whole family in a devastating tragedy, I couldn't help but wonder at his radiance as he opened this morning's service. His joy in loving and helping children was obvious. He had resigned from his job and was working full time with children Sunday after Sunday and summer after summer, traveling through rural communities to hold Bible schools. But how could he forgive the man who had murdered his own family?

As I reflected, I didn't see the girl who had bounced in and sat down beside me until she said breathlessly, "Hi, my name is Nancy. What's yours?"

She took me by surprise, and as I turned toward her I was caught up in the dazzle of her smile. Nancy was blond and pretty, but what made her different from other girls was that there was an immediate warmth about her and something intangible that reached out to me and held me captive. She had an upturned nose that added to her pert, saucy looks and dimples that dashed in and out of her cheeks. I found myself smiling and telling her my name.

Nancy held out a long, slim finger and whispered, "See my diamond? I just got engaged. His name is Steve, and he's in the army." She let it all out in one quick breath, and I couldn't help but smile as I examined her ring.

"Are you new here, too?" she asked.

"Heavens, no, I grew up in this place." I started to tell her that I was here because I had to be, that my parents were pillars of the church, and that I would prefer to be home sleeping.

Nancy was seventeen and like myself would be a senior in the fall. She was as blond as I was dark, and at that moment there was nothing in the world we had in common. She sat next to me in our little class, and we shared her Bible. When I saw the verses marked in red, I thought, "She really reads this!" She was obviously bright, and I couldn't imagine how she could find this dull, black book interesting.

When she was introduced to the class, her sunny face lit up. She was happy to find new friends so quickly, she said, looking right at me. Her openness was so obviously genuine I felt a tiny bit of ice melt in my heart.

Would I come to her home for dinner next Sunday? She said she would love to have me, and to my own surprise I readily gave her my telephone number.

That week certain thoughts kept racing through my mind: *She thinks I'm a Christian. If she really knew me, she wouldn't want me for dinner.* But because Sunday was usually an unexciting day and there was nothing better to do, it wouldn't matter one way or another.

Anyway, I knew all the right words and phrases and could bluff Nancy into believing I was a Christian. If, after spending one Sunday at her home, I didn't like her, I could just ignore her later on. But for now, what difference did one dinner at her home make?

15

Sunday afternoon found Nancy and me sitting cross-legged on her bed after a wonderful dinner. She told me about her fiance, Steve, and how she had met him while she was out bicycling one Saturday afternoon. Excitedly she showed me his pictures from faraway places, and we pored over them together.

Watching her happy face, I knew deep within that I had never experienced the kind of happiness and peace she had so obviously found.

Suddenly the words came tumbling out. I told her about Tom, about Sherry, about the rebellion in my heart toward everything that had to do with God and the church. I told her about Barry, raising that memory for only a moment, and then about April and how my mother had to devote every moment to her care. I talked about my father who didn't understand me at all after raising three boys. He had become linked with my concept of God — someone ready to zap me when I got out of line.

Nancy listened, leaning forward. Over and over I tossed my head and finished my sentences with "I wish things had been different." Finally my voice faltered and I bent my head, "I'm only seventeen and feel as though I've lived a lifetime."

Nancy didn't scold, preach, or moralize. She didn't say

anything at all, but behind her listening expression was an understanding heart. I knew without being told that she wanted to be my friend, and within my heart another piece of ice melted.

We went for a walk down the shady avenue. A breeze was stirring the budding leaves and lifting our hair to cool our faces. We talked but often were silent. I began to tell her how restless I had been ever since my brother had died and April had come to live with us. I told her that I had changed high schools hoping to find myself but that nothing had really changed. It seemed as though, I said, every time I found something to make me happy, it slipped through my fingers like melted butter. I wanted something permanent and lasting — was that so much to ask?

Nancy listened; and though she didn't have to say it, we both knew we were worlds apart in our thinking. She had found the peace I wanted so desperately, but I hoped she wouldn't tell me I had to be a Christian to find it.

Then I asked Nancy about all the do's and don'ts imposed on Christians, particularly teen-agers. We were walking home, and she stopped a moment to finger the leaf of a low-hanging branch.

"Like what?" she asked.

"You know — everything I love to do seems to be wrong." I couldn't go on to tell her about the many nights of leaning over a drink, smoking one cigarette after another. I said no more because Nancy was smiling.

"Do you remember what Jesus told His disciples when He called them?"

I knew, but I waited for her to continue.

"All He said was 'Follow Me.' "

"But where does that take you?" I whispered.

"Where are you now?"

We walked on silently. The sun was warming my face as I pondered that last question. Where was I? I was lost, confused, and lonely. Nancy seemed so sure of every step she took while I floundered along, stumbling through each day of my life.

Before I got into my Plymouth after thanking Nancy's parents, she said with a quiet smile, "What are you doing the Fourth of July? Wouldn't it be fun to go to Lake Michigan?"

It would be fun, I agreed, and waved good-by. For once in my life I had met someone who knew exactly where she was going. Nancy had listened to me pour out my innermost thoughts, understood, and then accepted me as a friend in spite of all I'd said.

I sat on the edge of my bed thinking about the day, feeling almost as if something important was going to happen to me. When nothing did, I went into the kitchen to help my mother start supper.

She didn't ask me about my day, but I found myself chatting happily about Nancy and her family. There was a new spring in my step, and when I felt a wave of tenderness toward April and carried on a conversation with her, I surprised even myself.

The sun was filtering through the venetian blinds, bathing my face in its promise of a perfect July day. The beach would be crowded on this national holiday, and hopefully the surf would be high. I scrambled through my closet for my shorts, pulled on a cool blouse, tied my long hair into a ponytail, and raced down the stairs. I still had that rising feeling of excitement that something was about to happen, and I was rushing out to meet it, whatever it could be.

I waved off my mother's offer of breakfast, jumped into my Plymouth, the convertible top down, and with the wind blowing through my hair, I drove over the hill to Nancy's house. She was waiting on the porch as I rolled into her driveway. She climbed into the car with a happy greeting.

"It's going to be a perfect day for the beach," I said, backing out.

"Do you mind," Nancy hesitated, and I stopped, "do you mind if another friend of mine comes along?"

I did mind but only for a moment, for just a block away we stopped to meet her friend Jennifer. Jennifer had straight brown hair that fell below her shoulders. Her eyes were a deep brown, and a double row of lashes made them appear even larger. She had a quiet, sedate beauty, and when she acknowledged the introduction she smiled directly at me, warm and welcoming. While Nancy and I talked, our sentences running into each other, Jennifer listened.

I was to find that Jennifer was one of those rare people who was born to be a listener, full of compassion and understanding. Nancy, vivacious and lively, matched my outgoing personality. Jennifer complemented us both.

Arriving at beautiful Lake Michigan, the water an azure blue and the waves high, we swam into the surf. Emerging, our hair hanging about our faces in wet strings, we gasped for breath. We dried ourselves and sunned into deep tans, then ran back into the water to cool off when the heat of the day became unbearable. We chatted like old friends, our three personalities melting as though that very day was meant to be.

We ate lunch at a small snack shop on the beach. The beach was filled with teen-agers and running children, but we were so busy getting to know each other we didn't even notice the crowd.

Jennifer told me about her mother who had died when she was only nine. Her father had remarried, and now her efforts in living the Christian life were meeting with opposition at home.

"How strange," I thought to myself. "She's struggling to live out her faith at home, and I'm struggling to run away from it."

"I've always thought that being a Christian was sort of like being in bondage." I said it slowly and thoughtfully because knowing these two happy girls made it no longer seem plausible.

"But it was Christ who came to set everyone *free*," Jennifer said softly. She seemed surprised that I didn't already know that.

"Free from what?" I leaned on my elbow.

Nancy answered with a quiet authority. "A person is a slave to whomever he serves, even if that person is himself. Do you understand?"

I thought of how it seemed impossible to break my old habits and half nodded.

"Christ came to set everyone free from the bondage of sin. When He does, only then are you really free."

I didn't like the word *sin*, so I remained quiet a moment. But the sad feeling arising within me confirmed that it was the only word that *could* be used. I squirmed and asked, "But what *is* sin? Is it going places and doing things you shouldn't?" I put my label on what I thought sin was, and Nancy smiled.

"Sin is separation from God. Adam started it all by disobeying God and running from Him. People have been born sinful ever since, so they can't help sinning. You know, the Bible says, "The heart [of man] is deceitful above all things, and desperately wicked' and that *all* have sinned and fall short of God's ideal."

I thought of my own deceitful heart and had to admit that I had lied and cheated and been dishonest. I often wondered why I couldn't stop when I wanted to. Now I was beginning to understand. *Of course* I had done all of those things, because that's the way people naturally are. *Is there no way out of myself?* I had asked a thousand times.

Nancy wasn't long in answering my unasked question. "God knew that man could never set himself free, so God Himself came in the person of Jesus Christ. Now by trusting in Him, we can be free from sin, from ourselves, from our old habits — free to walk within the circle of His love. He gives us freedom from guilt, freedom from fear, freedom to talk over our problems with Him. He knows, He cares, and He answers."

I liked the freedom-from-guilt part and said so. Jennifer and Nancy both agreed that to feel guilt was agonizing.

"It's funny," Nancy said wonderingly, "how people think that they can *do* something to win God's favor. You know, like keeping the Ten Commandments or trying harder to be good or working in the church or being baptized — when all the Lord wants from us is faith, repentance, and obedience."

"What about guilt?" I persisted.

Nancy carefully sifted sand through her fingers. "Do you remember the story of Moses when he was pleading with Pharaoh to let the children of Israel leave Egypt?"

I nodded. I remembered that one from Sunday school — the awful plagues, the exciting opening of the Red Sea, the journey in the wilderness.

Nancy continued, "Remember how the Israelites had to kill a lamb and apply the blood to the doorpost so that the angel of death would see it and pass over that home? It was their only escape from death. In exactly the same way *we* must apply the blood of the Lamb, Jesus Christ our Passover, to our lives. God sees that blood, and we too are saved from judgment. It was *their* only way out, and it is *our* only way out."

The blood applied to the Jewish doorposts . . . the blood applied to our hearts.

I had heard all of this before but I had never really understood.

"Just think, Jennifer spoke gently, "all of our sins are paid for. We only need to agree with God that we are sinners and put our faith in His death on the cross. When God sees the blood applied to our hearts, we are pardoned. Forever. Those who follow Christ are truly free and should be the happiest people in the world."

I didn't say anything. I was thinking about freedom from guilt. I wondered if it could be true that the weight on my heart could be lifted. I was thinking about freedom. What would it be like to be *really* free?

Nancy and Jennifer were silent, respecting my deep thoughts. When I looked up, they were watching me with clear looks of love, acceptance, and understanding. I hoped my voice would sound normal when I spoke.

"I never have to work at pleasing God? Is that what you are saying?"

Nancy smiled. "That's right. But you will *want* to please Him just as you want to please anyone you love. In the obedience comes great peace and joy. If you're feeling guilty, may I say something?"

I nodded, looking down.

"It's because you *are*."

Nancy looked so sad for me that I couldn't argue the point. I did feel guilty — more guilty than ever. I was facing something I couldn't handle, and my heart felt both heavy and light at the same time.

We lay on the beach until the sun began to hide behind a glowing red sunset.

"Of course," Nancy continued, "there is something you must know."

"I *do* know," I said in a muffled tone. "I've got to believe."

"And receive. Remember how the children of Israel had to *look* at the serpent Moses held up in order to be healed?"

I remembered.

"Unless they *looked*, they died," Nancy said. "And it's still the same, unless you look at the Cross and receive the forgiveness offered for your sins, you too will be under God's death penalty."

"It sounds so harsh." I had often thought that, and it felt good to say it. It was almost like telling God.

"It is harsh to the unbeliever, but sweet to the one who receives. Remember? God gave us a way out. Faith in Jesus Christ, and in His death, burial, and resurrection, is the answer."

I didn't want to talk about it any more. I knew I was being faced with the personal decision of what *I* would do about looking at that Cross.

I didn't know. I couldn't think. I had *never* wanted to be a Christian. That meant forgiving God for all the mistakes and hurts He had caused me. That meant accepting my parents' faith and admitting I had been wrong. I didn't want to face this moment yet, but it was causing an aching hurt inside.

We drove home in thoughtful silence. As I pulled my

Plymouth into our wide driveway, I was glad no one else was at home. I wanted to be alone.

I washed the sand out of my hair and, sitting before my dressing table, leaned forward and looked at myself in the oval mirror. Were those tears in my eyes? Was I crying tears of relief and happiness? Or were they tears of sadness that I had spent so many wasted years chasing an elusive joy?

The room was still. Twilight had deepened into night. Suddenly I was on my knees. Great sobs were welling up from within as I cried the words aloud: "God, I do want You! I want You to come into my life. Lord, forgive me — forgive me — forgive me. Take this life that I've messed up — please make something good out of it. And I cried the same words over and over, kneeling there weeping until a perfect cleansing washed over me. I knew I was free at last.

I finally crawled into bed, and as I drifted off to sleep, my mind felt as though a fresh breeze had captured it. I wanted to call Nancy and Jennifer and shout over the telephone wires that I was *free*. But instead I just lay there, letting the One who promised to carry my burdens lift them from me and wash me clean with His precious blood.

⚜ 16 ⚜

When dawn came streaming through my window, I remembered the joy of the night before, and a thousand questions rose to greet me.

I would be a senior in the fall. Would I be able to share my new faith with my friends? And what would they think? What about dear Laurie who was so sweet and kind to everyone? Would she wonder what in the world I was talking about? I was sure she felt she was as good as anyone and didn't need religion. And she *was* good. But how could I tell her that good in man's eyes was not good in God's eyes? Would I be able to?

What about Janie and her crowd? I had been a regular at their weekend parties, some of them a lot wilder than I cared to remember. What would they think of me? Would they laugh and ridicule? And in such a small school, wouldn't everyone notice if I changed *too* much? Could I *really* follow the Lord? Did I really *want* to?

I thought of my old life. I knew what was back there. I didn't want that. There was only one place to go and that was forward. I had tried over and over to do it on my own and couldn't. I had to have God on my side. There was no other choice.

I sank to my knees and whispered, "Lord — " How

easily that Name came to my lips now! " — last night I gave
my life to You. I want to reaffirm that promise this morning.
Wherever it takes me, I need Your love, forgiveness, and
direction. You promised never to leave me. I'm counting on
that, Father." Father. God was my *Father*. My loving, kind,
patient, forgiving, *heavenly* Father.

I was ready now to go downstairs and share with my
parents that at last I was a new person in Christ. There would
be no more unkept promises. No more turning over of new
leaves. I knew that now it would not be me living this
brand-new life but "Christ in me."

I was about to embark on a new life, and the excitement
was impossible to hide. I told my mother first, and soon tears
were falling from our eyes.

"Honey," she said quietly, "I've been waiting for this
moment since the day you were born. I promised the Lord
when I knew I was going to have another baby that this one
would be all His. I surrendered you to Him while you were
still within me."

I hugged April, who smiled up at me with shining eyes.
How *could* I have been so selfish as to resent this little girl
who was suffering so much physical pain? "Christ in me" was
beginning to love little April.

I told my dad, asking him to forgive me for my attitude
of coldness and distance. Tension melted, and my dad became my dear, loving, forgiving father. He knew his days of
heartache and worry about me were over.

Nancy was the next person I called, and I had the
feeling she already knew. She would be over soon, she said,
was it all right? *Was* it!

Then I called Jennifer, and I knew by the silence on the
other end of the line that she was weeping with joy.

Sunday was bright and gloriously awash with a summer
rain. With Nancy and Jennifer on one side of me and my
parents and April on the other side, I couldn't stop the tears

sliding down my cheeks. God my Father was filling me with an inner peace and surrounding me with love — His love, which was eternal and divine, and the love of His children to help me in my new walk with Him.

My new life had just begun!

17

> I waited patiently for the Lord; and he inclined unto me, and heard my cry. He brought me up also out of an horrible pit, out of the miry clay, and set my feet upon a rock, and established my goings. And he put a new song in my mouth, even praise unto our God: many shall see it, and fear, and shall trust in the Lord (Ps. 40:1-3 KJV).

What beautiful, wondrous words penned by David, the king of ancient Israel! I was sure they had been written just for me.

My home, which had seemed like a prison in the past, became a haven. The sky appeared blue even when it was gray, and the tree outside my window looked like the most glorious creation in all the world. I no longer needed to listen to the songs of the "blues," for I had a new song in my heart, and I felt as if I could burst with joy. I wanted to tell anyone who would listen.

My old friends had been taken from me, some through death, but God was filling my life with Himself, and because He knew I would need company on my new journey, He gave me the companionship of Nancy and Jennifer.

My old habits slid out of my life as I began to sing new songs to my God. The language that had fallen from my lips bringing dishonor to God's name disappeared. My old desires were gone, replaced by new goals and joys. I no longer had to prove that I was grown up and sophisticated. I knew now that I wasn't. I was simply a seventeen-year-old girl who had just "been born."

Before my own eyes the mask of hardened indifference melted away. In its place was a fresh, new "me" who actually sparkled with joy.

Words poured from my heart onto paper:

> I was playing a role
> In a real life drama,
> A mechanical smiling
> Real moving actor,
> Saying the right lines
> At the right time.
>
> While deep inside me
> Were dark and desperate thoughts
> Of hurt toward my fellow actors,
> A line misunderstood,
> A stance out of place
> Sent signals of bitterness
> To my breaking, wounded soul.
>
> I played my role well
> And won an award
> Of favor from my fellow players,
> Such a nice person
> Such a good spirit,
> Such a help in need,
> While inside raged another.
>
> I took off my mask
> One day by chance
> And looked into the mirror
> To see a face unlike my own,
> Furrowed lines, wrinkled brow,
> Tightened lips
> Had grown under the smiling facade.
>
> I threw the mask away
> And opened the windows of my soul

And let God's Spirit reach deep
Into my own.
He found the real me
Underneath the guise
And cleansed me from bitterness
And hung me out to dry
In His sunshine,
And when His light shone through
I was whole.

That summer delightful joys crept into my heart. Many evenings, propped up in bed with my Bible, I read and reread the words of Jesus. I thought I had known the Bible, but I had only known words. Now I understood with my spirit.

I walked with Jesus through the Book of John, and my heart quickened as He talked gently to Nicodemus, the righteous ruler of the Jews, telling him firmly, "You must be born again." I nodded fiercely. Now I knew why it was a *must*. The old me couldn't make it and neither could the old Nicodemus.

I loved the story of the woman at the well. I felt the compassion of the Lord as He waited there in the sun, weary from a long day's journey. He had an appointment with this woman at this hour and nothing would stand in His way. So He waited. I watched as she approached the well, her face registering disbelief that He, a Jewish rabbi, would speak to her, a woman and a despised Samaritan at that. The disbelief turned to wonder as He told her what He had made known to no one else as yet — that He was the Messiah. He stated with authority, "Whoever drinks of the water that I shall give him shall never thirst." Tears stood in my eyes as I looked after the woman, running to the town and leaving her water pot at the well. Yes, she had good news to tell her townspeople. I almost ran with her as she shouted, "Come, see a man, who told me all things that ever I did."

I knew that I, too, would never thirst again as long as I drank deeply of the water of life, Jesus Christ. I would never again have to chase after the things of this world — never again. That thought thrilled my heart.

When I entered the fourteenth chapter of John it was with an expectant heart. I read the words again, letting them sink into my mind: "Peace I leave with you; My peace I give to you; not as the world gives, do I give to you. Let not your heart be troubled, nor let it be fearful" (v. 27 NAS).

I marveled as Jesus comforted His troubled disciples, though He Himself was on the way to the cross. His own bitter cup was set aside for a moment while He brought solace to their sorrowing, fearful hearts.

"And I will ask the Father, and He will give you another Helper, that He may be with you forever; *that is* the Spirit of truth, whom the world cannot receive, because it does not behold Him or know Him, *but* you know Him because He abides with you, and will be in you. I will not leave you as orphans; I will come to you (vv. 16-18). But sadly they could not understand.

John 15, the "abiding chapter," filled my heart with the joy that Jesus promised: "These things I have spoken to you, that My joy may be in you, and that your joy may be made full" (v. 11). What a word to use as He faced the agonizing death of the cross: *Joy*. Yes, He said it would be *full* joy. I imagined the Eleven listening in astonishment as He spoke of their coming joy. Little could these bewildered men dream that the joy of the Lord would be their strength and that it would carry them through persecution, imprisonment, and finally martyrdom.

I read the prayer of Jesus aloud in my room, feeling His love as He cried out "Holy Father, keep through thine own name those whom thou hast given me, that they may be one as we are [one]" (John 17:11 KJV). At last I understood God's plan for the human race: that we might know God and Jesus Christ whom He sent; that we might receive Him and love Him and obey Him; that we might love one another as God poured His love through us by His Holy Spirit.

I watched Him with His disciples on the seashore after His resurrection. How beautiful, I thought, that He should not only supply their breakfast but cook it for them, all the while calming their fears.

I closed the Book of John and hugged it to me. True living water was contained within these pages, enough to satisfy the thirst of the whole world.

It was no wonder that my mother could serve April patiently and tenderly, for she had heard the words of Jesus: "Whoever receives one child like this in My name is receiving Me" (Mark 9:37 NAS). No wonder death couldn't confound my parents or Uncle Paul, for hadn't Jesus Himself said, "Because I live, you shall live also" (John 1:19 NAS)?

The summer of my eighteenth year became a springboard for my new faith. I was determined to start my last year of high school, not turning over a new leaf, but living a new life.

I slipped once more to my knees and named each one of my friends by name.

Kate — Dear Lord, bring her to You.

Marie — How sweet she is, Lord; may she find You precious.

And dear Laurie — Help me show her the road to You.

Sherry — Tears flooded my eyes, and once more I thanked God for letting Sherry hear the good news of life in Jesus Christ before she died. And as the tears flooded my bedspread, I whispered Tom's name over and over. "O Lord, I pray that Tom may have come to know You before the ocean swallowed him in its depths. I promise, Lord, I'll never fail another friend. I promise I'll tell everyone about You. . . . I promise. . . . I promise. . . ."

18

The summer of '43. . . . Nancy, Jennifer, and I pooled our gas stamps and made our way to Gull Lake for one beautiful, carefree month. We rented an old cottage on the lakeshore, complete with a dilapidated rowboat we could call our own for the whole time we were there.

Often we rowed out into the middle of the lovely blue water to swim in the clear waves around our anchored boat. The lake was rightfully named, for tiny gulls would sweep down gracefully on the rippling waters.

One day when we were rowing around the long bend, we caught sight of a huge sailboat filled with boys. The war had seemingly taken all the males our own age, so we rowed closer for a better look. We had discovered the gorgeous Kellogg Estate which was being used as a rehabilitation center for returning veterans. The young men, seeing three girls, began to whistle and wave frantically.

We docked our small boat and toured the expansive grounds with the recuperating veterans. They told us about their war experiences, and standing next to a boy who had lost an arm or leg made the war become very real. The horrors of war became vividly impressed on our minds.

We stood on a picturesque bridge for hours and chatted with the homesick servicemen. As we shared our faith in God, some listened intently and some not at all. We saw courage; we saw bitterness. From them we learned far more about the war on the other side of the world than we could have known in any other way.

"See those guys over there?" one soldier said at one point, and we turned to watch two young men pruning bushes, their faces carefully turned from us. "German prisoners," he shrugged. We stared at their bent blond heads. *German prisoners? Really?* But they were so young, and they looked like anyone who might have sat next to us in school. How could *they* be our enemy? It was a startling moment for Nancy, Jennifer, and me, a moment we would never forget.

When our month was over, we sadly said good-by, snapping pictures of them hanging out of their sailboats or standing on the shores. We were silent as we rowed back around the bend, but it was time to go home again.

September's golden days arrived along with the beginning of a new semester at school. For Nancy and Jennifer it would be another year like the previous ones. But for me it would be totally different. I would have to walk into an old situation as a new person. I couldn't do it on my own, so I prayed fervently the night before school started and repeated God's promise to me. He had said, "I will never leave you nor forsake you." I knew He wouldn't.

And He didn't. For as I awoke on Monday morning all fear and apprehension vanished. I ate breakfast in our sunny nook, kissed my mother good-by, and walked the short block to the bus stop as I had six months before.

But this time I had a Friend by my side.

Climbing onto the bus, I found Laurie in her usual place. She smiled her welcome for me to join her. I hadn't seen her all summer, and her smile brought a grin to my face. I wanted Laurie to be the first friend I would tell of my new life. I didn't know how to begin, so I waited until the right moment. Then I heard myself saying, "Laurie, something wonderful has happened to me. May I tell you about it?"

Laurie nodded, looking deeply into my eyes.

"You're in love," she laughed.

I smiled. "Something like that. Laurie, I met the two most wonderful friends this summer, but that isn't the best part. They showed me what it's like to be a real Christian. I mean, I came to know Jesus Christ this summer and, well, I do love Him now with my whole heart. I'm a new person, Laurie, a really new person."

"I can tell," she said quietly.

"Really? Can you?" I hugged my books to me and fell silent.

Laurie glanced at me sideways and said thoughtfully, "Well, you're not going to change *too* much, are you? I hope you're not going to be a religious fanatic or anything like that. I mean, we always had a lot of fun together, and I'd sure miss that."

"Laurie, we're going to have a lot more fun, just wait and see. As for religious? No — I've just met the Lord personally, and He's given me a new purpose in life — a whole new outlook on everything."

Laurie looked a little skeptical, and I knew I would just have to show her the kind of purpose and joy a follower of Jesus Christ could have — just the way Nancy and Jennifer had shown me.

Soon we were back in the old corridors, shouting at our friends and cramming our books into our lockers as we headed for first period and civics class. The whole senior class met for two hours, and because it was the first day of school it took some time for us to settle down for our adored teacher, Miss Flannigan.

When Janie asked me to one of her weekend parties, I smiled and said, "No, I couldn't go along with that crowd any more." I explained to a first puzzled then indifferent Janie that I had something more satisfying.

One day when I was reading my little New Testament in homeroom, Janie turned around and said so loud that everyone could hear, "That's foolishness."

For a moment I didn't know what to say, but I had just been reading a verse that fit perfectly. I held the Bible for her to see, "Why Janie, look here. I was just reading about you."

She was disdainful. "About me? Don't be silly."

"Yes, just listen to this." I read it to her: "For the word of the cross is to those who are perishing foolishness, but to us who are being saved it is the power of God" (1 Cor. 1:18 NAS).

She stared, a coolness sweeping over her eyes before she turned her back on me. I never had to worry about Janie and her crowd any more. She never spoke to me again.

That year Nancy was awarded the lead in the senior play at her school. Acting sounded like fun, and though I hadn't done any before, I decided to try out for our school's play. Amazingly, when I tried out for the comedy *Out of the Frying Pan,* I won one of the three leading parts.

"You seem to be just the girl for this part," the drama teacher said, looking at me thoughtfully. "I watched you around school last year, and you seemed to be quite sophisticated."

I was to play a worldly wise, sophisticated, movie-struck girl aspiring to be an actress. The name of the girl I would play? Kate! I played her well because I had known and loved someone just like her and had lived in her shadow for a long time.

It was exhilarating. The long nights of rehearsals, the excitement of opening night, the comaraderie of the cast, and the resounding applause. I loved every minute of it. The play was a success and was highly acclaimed by our local newspaper. When we were invited to stage it at Camp Custer for the soldiers, we were thrilled.

And I had an opportunity to share my faith with all the kids in the play about my new life in Christ.

"Lord," I prayed after the play was over, "that was great, but now I want a chance to tell the whole senior class about You. Somehow, some way, let me be able to explain fully and clearly what You mean to me. Let me erase my past by my new life."

God gave me a unique opportunity. One day in a class

discussion, everyone was giving his own view of the world situation. Conversation lingered and debates were lengthy about the war, what to do with the Nazis when the war was won, and about the state of President Roosevelt's health. Everyone was given equal time to share his view on any subject at all. Suddenly from within I heard one forceful word: "Now."

"Now, Lord? Are You sure?"

"Now is your last chance. Speak for Me now."

I began to tremble all over, but the next moment I was standing up and asking Miss Flannigan if I could share something that had happened to me. Always gracious, she smiled her accord.

I don't remember everything I said, but I do remember starting out with these words: "Maybe you kids wonder what happened to me this year. You knew me before as a very unsettled girl who was out of school a lot. You knew that my language wasn't — well, what it should have been." I paused and swallowed. "You know now that I'm a new person, and I'd like to tell you why."

I told the class that I had been running from authority. I told them that I found that God had given His life for mine so that I might be free. "It's an exchanged life," I explained. "He's been the answer to my years of searching and He can be yours too."

When I concluded and sat down, the class was unusually silent. I saw tears standing in Laurie's eyes.

"I did it, Lord," I said silently.

"*You* stood up," I heard within my heart, "but *I* did it. You allowed yourself to be My channel, and from now on that's all I want you to do. Just stand up and let Me speak through you."

I could only whisper a weak thank-you to my heavenly Father through lips that still trembled.

The class went on to other discussions that day, but I felt as though I had not only done that for Jesus Christ but I had also shared my faith for my friends whom I had failed — my long-lost friends Tom and Sherry.

❧ 19 ❧

That day became a springboard for sharing my faith with my classmates one by one. Often I was challenged and ridiculed, yet several searching hearts found the balm of Jesus Christ to be their healing.

I will always remember Nora. She was our class valedictorian, and somehow it "just happened" that Nora and I had lunch together at the Coffee Cup for several days in succession.

"I'm an atheist," she stated proudly, "and I'll tell you why." Nora talked on and on about why she had reasoned that there was no God. I watched, fascinated at her brilliant rhetoric but wondering just how God was going to move her stubborn heart.

I simply shared my own life and what Christ had meant in bringing me peace. I told her about my restlessness and she smiled a little smugly. "It's all psychological," she told me with patience, as if talking to a simple-minded child. "You see, because you needed a change, it came about. I don't need one."

And it really didn't seem as though she did. She was the top student in our class, popular, and a talented musician. There seemed to be no doubt that Nora would become a success.

But when I opened my yearbook and read what Nora wrote, I smiled at the ways of God: "You'll never know what our talks at the Coffee Cup have meant to me. They made me start thinking. Thank you for caring."

Nora was a miracle. Whenever I meet someone whom I think will never turn to God, I think of her. Two years after graduation Nora met the living Lord face to face, married, and became a missionary, with her husband, to South America. She truly was a success, but not in the way she thought she would be. God met her and captured her heart as only He could.

Laurie and I remained close friends. There would always be a special place in my heart for her. She had loved me when I was "lost" and continued to love me when I was "found." The day would come when Laurie would experience a breaking heart on the edge of a broken life and whisper, "I too have turned my life over to God."

As I remembered my promise not to fail another friend, God gave me many opportunities to share my faith. At class parties, on lunch hours, or even in the halls between classes, I was able to tell my classmates, one by one, about God's love.

When we seniors were asked to write out our philosophy of life, I could hear the whisper in my heart, "Now you have a chance to let your teachers know what I have done for you."

So my term paper became my testimony. First I told about my happy childhood, then of the sudden death of my brother, my resentment over the adoption of his daughter, and my other unhappy losses. Finally I wrote: "But then I met my Savior." Page after page, I explained how my life was changed from chaos to peace and what Jesus meant to me. I ended my paper with the words: "Thank you, Mrs. Walker, for letting me come to Oakdale High."

When my paper was returned, I found that the lovely principal had written across the bottom of the last page of my composition, "How sweet of you, and I'm glad you came to Oakdale."

Leaving the familiar halls of high school for the last time was a bittersweet experience. We spent the last day at school running through the corridors signing each other's yearbooks and writing honestly to each other, perhaps because we knew, for some of us at least, we might never meet again.

On graduation night Nora, brilliant in her valedictorian speech, bade farewell for all of us. We sat tearfully through the ceremonies, then the blue robes were removed and the caps laid aside. We wept together, hugging each other and promising that we would keep in touch, all the while somehow knowing we wouldn't.

That summer, Nancy, Jennifer, and I spent a month basking in the sun on Lake Michigan. We had a one-room cabin not far from the beaches, and from early dawn until twilight we lay near the water enjoying every precious moment of our last carefree days.

I remember one night so clearly. The stars were twinkling beside a full moon, and the trees by our cabin were stirring only slightly in the warm summer night. We stood on a wooden pier looking out over the vast lake, and it was Jennifer who said softly, "I wonder what life will be like for us ten years from this very night." Nancy and I reflected with her, trying to project ourselves into such *old* people of almost *thirty*.

"Well — the war will be over for one thing." I offered.

"Maybe — " Nancy sighed, twisting her diamond. She hadn't seen Steve in two full years.

The war had taken up most of our teen years, and we had lived with it so long it seemed a natural part of our lives.

Jennifer went on, "We'll probably be married and have babies and a home of our own, don't you think?"

It was still the American dream. A small home with a white picket fence and a wide green yard surrounding it. Marriage and babies and living happily ever after was still the way we wanted our stories to end.

Pollution and inflation and drugs and population explosion and women's liberation were for another era. These were problems our children would have to face. But we still clung with all of our fanciful dreams to romantic castle-building. Somewhere there was a handsome knight on a white horse, and he'd come riding into our lives and sweep us off our feet, and we'd fall madly in love and marry him and it would be forever. That was the whimsical dream of our times, and that's just the way it was.

"And we'll still be best friends." Nancy said firmly. "probably just as silly and having just as much fun as we are now."

We agreed, but something stirred uneasily, whispering that maybe things would change and we might have to move apart. We stood on that long wooden pier just dreaming and wishing. Finally we turned in silence and walked through the winding narrow path under the starry sky to our cabin.

It was a happy, sad, unforgettable night.

When August was over, we headed back for the city — Nancy and Jennifer to secretarial positions and I to await confirmation of whether I was accepted as a student at Moody Bible Institute in Chicago.

The telegram finally came announcing my acceptance, and I could hardly contain my excitement. *Wouldn't it be just like heaven to be in a school with all Christian kids?* I thought as I packed. There would be no problems at all. I said good-by to my friends and prepared for the long drive to Chicago and my first semester at Moody.

Somehow in my new experience as a Christian I hadn't learned that when one is born into God's family, he is born as a baby. I didn't know that a new Christian must grow just as a baby does, little by little. I hadn't learned that growing is often experienced through heartache, and I had never learned about God's "pruning the branches." Nor did I know that He often uses other people to chip away at our rough edges. I had no idea that all my years of pride and selfishness would have to be pruned away.

I knew nothing of hardships or trials. Since I had come to the Lord, my path had been gloriously bright. I had my own car and my own checkbook. Chicago appeared to be only a continuation of my abundantly happy life.

I had just completed a thrilling year of sharing my new faith, and God had allowed some fruit in my life. But wouldn't it be much easier to be with others of similar faith? And wouldn't they love me just the way I was?

20

It was a cool September day when I had my first glimpse of Chicago. We drove through the steel town of Gary, Indiana, then through the south side, and finally onto the Outer Drive along beautiful Lake Michigan. I was silent in the back seat as my brother Stephen maneuvered the car through the busy streets. The buildings were tall and imposing, and my heart sank deeper and deeper as we made our way into the heart of the city.

Moody Bible Institute, with its huge stone arches, was a formidable cement structure in the midst of narrow streets and dingy shops. There were no green acres of campus. In fact, there was hardly a reedy tree bending in the wind. The picture was far from inviting.

My heart dropped still further as my brother pulled into the small parking lot of Institute Place. I was directed to my room two blocks away, next to the Masonic Temple, where "dancing went on all night." The dormitories were old, and there was no air conditioning — I couldn't imagine what my small room must be like on hot, humid days. It all looked so unfamiliar and depressing that I almost bolted for the door.

What am I doing here? I kept asking myself as I envisioned my pink-and-white bedroom at home, with its large closet and private bath. My mother, as accustomed to luxury as I, looked stricken as we said our good-bys. I felt deserted as I watched my parents' Buick pull away, and when it disappeared from sight, I fought tears of loneliness.

Suddenly a smiling face appeared in my doorway, and I met my first new friend. Her name was Mary Anne, and her southern drawl and quick wit sent me into gales of laughter. Like me, she had come from an affluent background, and I was grateful to the Lord for bringing her into my life at that moment.

I wondered with Mary Anne about the school's regulations. We had both let down our skirts to the proper length, but what most worried me was getting up at six o'clock in the morning for chapel. Mary Anne promised to see that I was up; and at 5:30 the next morning, she burst into my room, plugged the drain in the sink, and started the tap water. I was forced to get up or face a small flood.

Thus I began to make my way through the mountain of rules, tests, papers, and morning chapel hour. My "pruning" had begun.

I'm sure I didn't endear myself to some of my fellow students. Many were struggling to pay for their next month's room and board, while I had my own checking account, cash in my purse, and a full-length fur coat for "special" occasions. It must have been especially disconcerting for them whenever I walked into the dining room, looked at the menu, and left with a friend or two for a nearby restaurant. My pattern of living had been so deeply ingrained that it never occurred to me to "gird myself with humility" and walk in step with my daily companions.

So I learned an important lesson the time a group of us were assigned to pick up some inner-city children for Sunday school. The tenement buildings, decrepit and ancient, had narrow staircases, broken steps, and odors I had never known existed. Open garbage cans sent my senses reeling as I climbed flight after flight of wooden stairs. *I can do it, I can do it*, I repeated to myself until finally I knew I could. While my stomach rebelled at the sights, smells, and sounds, urging me to run from these places, I kept going until, to my surprise, I found myself actually looking forward to Sunday.

I had fallen in love with the inner-city children, holding their hands as we skipped down Chicago Avenue on the way to Sunday school.

I remember so well the faces of hostile parents — unhappy, confused, frightened faces. I remember the sadness in children's eyes as they stood there, hungry, with torn, threadbare clothes, many of them without coats and shoes.

Poverty was everywhere — poverty of the soul as well as material impoverishment. I was dizzy with guilt, thinking of my checkbook, which never ran out of funds, and of my bulging wardrobe. I stumbled through those tenement houses with mixed feelings of pity and helplessness.

On campus my classes were challenging, but the class I enjoyed most was the one I took under Dr. Smith. I listened with rapt attention to his teachings, realizing more fully that I could draw strength in every situation from an all-powerful Source — God's Holy Spirit. I was released from struggling to live my life on my own power, from trying hard to be good, and I learned I could trust God to work in me and through me.

Yet as I became involved with my studies, projects, and new friends, I found I had neglected my promise to tell others about God's love and all He had done for me. Then my friend Bill told me something I have never forgotten: "Sometimes we get so busy learning to be a Christian worker that we forget how to be a Christian." I wanted to remember forever my first calling — to "know Him" and to be completely His.

I was learning, too, that God does not *suggest* that we obey Him; He *commands* it. He does not say it would be nice if we would learn to love each other; He *demands* that we love one another *even as He loved us*. As I was considering the impossibility of that command, another verse came to mind with a sweet promise: "Because the love of God has been poured out within our hearts through the Holy Spirit who was given to us" (Rom. 5:5 NAS). *God* would love *through me*.

God was also "pruning" me through ordinary things like keeping my room clean, getting to class on time, remembering to go on my assignments, and learning to understand and love people from different cultures. I had wanted to do something extra special for God in some exotic, faraway place while He wanted me to obey Him in the "small" things right where I was.

There were many exciting things to do in and around Chicago. When we wanted to escape the noise of the big city, a group of us would head for Lake Michigan, where we could walk along sandy white beaches and enjoy the expanse of water. We barbecued on the beach and sat in huddled groups on moonlit evenings, gazing at the star-filled skies above.

Sometimes we would take the El to the suburban town of Wheaton. The sprawling homes, acres of green lawns, and lovely elms filled our longing for the natural beauty of the countryside. There in the winter we ice-skated on the lagoon, half-hidden by the trees. The small college town became an oasis from the busyness and noises of downtown Chicago.

But the heart of the city fascinated me. I loved window-shopping along Michigan Avenue, stopping to purchase items in small, exquisite shops. By the time I went Christmas shopping alone in the Loop, the magic of Chicago had captured my heart. Nancy and Jennifer made weekend trips to visit me, and together we explored the restaurants and shops or simply rode the clanging El, trying to capture all the sights of the city.

During the second semester I had an assignment at the Pacific Garden Mission on Skid Row. As I walked past the masses of people who sat along the curb in isolated dejection, I wondered where they all came from and whether they had families. The unshaven men sitting gloomily on hard benches smelling of liquor reminded me of the "innocent" drinks I had had at parties in the past. If God hadn't intervened, would I have spent my life sitting on a bench doing nothing, thinking nothing? Could we or anyone else reach these lonely people with the Good News of God's love in a way they would be able to understand?

My second semester was almost over when, on a bright April morning, our nation was rocked with the sad news, "Our president is dead!" Franklin Delano Roosevelt, the only president I had ever known, the only president I had ever seen, was dead. I felt a deep personal loss. Who was Harry Truman? And could he provide the strong leadership our nation needed during these final desperate days of the worldwide war?

Victory in Europe came in early June and with it the confident hope that Japan would soon surrender.

At the same time that these events were shaking our nation and the world, my spiritual life took an important turn in quite an unexpected way. On an ordinary morning in chapel, a guest speaker stood at the podium to address the students. Once he began to speak, I felt he was there just for me.

"What about unanswered questions that face us constantly? How do we as Christians answer when we are faced with the questions of why God permits a child to be born crippled or why He allows a person cut down in the bloom of his life? What about the boys who have been killed or maimed in the war? How do we answer their loved ones who are crying why? What about sickness that ravishes our bodies leaving us weak and shaken?"

My questions — the ones I had had since I was a child. Somehow they had never been answered to my satisfaction.

The professor went on. "Why does God allow devastating wars when He promised peace?"

Yes, why? my heart echoed.

"God is God." He emphasized each word. *"His thoughts are not our thoughts nor His ways our ways.* He does not have to explain His ways. Has God ever promised that we wouldn't have to suffer? No, but He did promise strength for each trial. God did not promise peace to the world until the Prince of Peace, Jesus Christ Himself, returns; but He did promise peace to the individual heart.

Now, listen carefully. For every question in your heart, give back the answer of — " he paused while I waited breathlessly — "*praise*. Yes, the answer is praise.

"You see, God is interested in conforming *you* to the image of His Son. He knows the road He must let you travel so that *you* may become like Jesus. Whenever God permits trials in your life, it is to bring glory to Himself and to let you experience growth. Of course often we bring about our own trials and heartaches by disobedience and sin, but even so, if we are truly His children, then 'all things work together for good to them that love God.' "

Then the professor told the story of Joseph, making it come alive again. Sold into slavery at the young age of seventeen, taken from his beloved father, imprisoned for a crime he didn't commit, his good name slandered, Joseph could have shaken his fist at God and screamed, "Why? I did nothing to deserve this." But Joseph waited patiently for the Lord, and in His own time God exalted Joseph to become prime minister of the country where he had been imprisoned. Ultimately Joseph saved not only his family, but the whole nation of Israel. Later Joseph could say to his brothers, "You meant evil against me, but God meant it for good" (Gen. 50:20 NAS).

"That's the secret." The teacher's eyes gleamed. "Though our enemy brings evil and means to make us stumble, God turns *all* things to good if we let Him."

Then the professor told the story of David — how he had to hide in caves from Saul, how his own children betrayed him, how his enemies pursued him, and — suddenly the professor's voice rose to a crescendo — "yet David could write the beautiful words: 'I will bless the Lord at all times: his praise shall continually be in my mouth.' "

At *all* times? I listened thoughtfully as the speaker continued, reminding us of the apostle Paul's tender letters to the churches, admonishing them "in everything give thanks; for this is God's will for you in Christ Jesus" (1 Thess. 5:18 NAS).

Later that night I sat at my desk with my forehead

resting in the palm of my hand. I don't know how long I sat there, but dusk had settled over the city and the clanging noises of LaSalle Street had become more subdued as my thoughts whirled around and around.

Could it be true? Should we praise God in *everything? Could it be* that God could turn Uncle Paul's tragic loss into something good? It had hardly seemed possible to me as a child, desperately trying to understand how God could let that family be murdered. But I thought of Uncle Paul's devotion to bringing children to Jesus Christ. When the records were revealed in eternity, how many thousands of boys and girls would have come to know the Lord because of this one man who hadn't let tragedy defeat him, but who had let God turn evil into good?

Could it be that April would bring more praise to God and fulfill His purpose as she was then if she were physically whole? *Could it be* that God was using April in our home to teach my impulsive, always-in-a-hurry father patience? *Could it be* that He wanted to prove His grace sufficient to my mother so her life could be an inspiration to others who watched in awe as she tenderly cared for April's needs? *Could it be* that April was needed as a light in the orthopedic wards and children's hospitals, where there was so much suffering, to bring her witness of Jesus Christ?

Who could resist the smiling girl on crutches looking up and telling of her faith? April had captured the hearts of the doctors and nurses and let her world know that God's grace was sufficient even through intense suffering. *Could it be* that April would bring more glory to God and witness more to His sustaining power than my strong, healthy brother Barry would have done had he lived?

Could it be that Sherry never would have listened to a pastor sitting at her bedside speaking quietly of God's love and forgiveness if she had not been in the last hours of her life?

Could it be — and tears were flowing freely now — that on a navy ship surrounded by miles of water that Tom was gently guided to the God he had often thought about?

Could it really be possible to praise God for all those unanswered heartaches and leave it to Him to turn all things to good? Would offering the sacrifice of praise really lay to rest forever the questions that were still in my heart?

Throughout the night I hugged this truth to me like a golden nugget — a truth new to me but as ancient as God's Word. Job said it: "Though he slay me, yet will I trust him." David said it: "My expectation is from the Lord. I shall *yet* have reason to praise him." Paul said it: "For our light affliction, which is but for a moment, worketh for us a far more exceeding and eternal weight of glory" (2 Cor. 4:17 KJV). And the writer to the Hebrews summed it all up: "All discipline for the moment seems not to be joyful, but sorrowful; yet to those who have been trained by it, afterwards it yields the peaceful fruit of righteousness" (Heb. 12:11 NAS).

I knew that I must give God my continual praise, for *He* was painting the picture and knew the end from the beginning, just as my mother had tried to explain to me years before.

I knelt at the foot of my bed — at the foot of the cross really — and began to thank God for every hurt that had come into my life, at first in halting words, then in bursting psalms of praise. As dawn spread across the city, the comforting words of Isaiah covered my newly cleansed heart and embedded themselves there forever: "Thou [God] wilt keep him in perfect peace, whose mind is stayed on thee: because he trusteth in thee" (Isa. 26:3 KJV).

He has! He does! He will!

21

The war was over! Japan had surrendered unconditionally. Yet almost every block in our town had a star in someone's window, sadly reflecting the price of the long conflict.

As I swung aimlessly on the porch swing that sweltering summer day, I thought of all the boys I knew who wouldn't be coming home — boys from high school — Bob, Jim, Sonny, football stars, trumpet players, and laughing boys gone forever. But tears came with thoughts of Tom. I knew I would have to turn that memory over once and for all and claim God's "perfect peace."

Only two years before I had claimed boldly, "I surrender my life to Christ." I wondered now if maybe I should have said, "I *am* surrendering my life to Christ." I was learning that it was a moment-by-moment, day-by-day walk, for memories had a way of coming alive at the most unexpected moments. Old patterns popped up every so often in spite of vows to "be better." I clung to God's promise, "As thy days so shall thy strength be" (Deut. 33:25 KJV).

I didn't want to look back — I knew what was there. I didn't want to look ahead — I didn't know what the future would hold. I wanted to live only today in the power of God's strength.

I let the porch swing gently rock me. I was still crying. I thought about the boys I had dated at Moody — once nearly getting engaged — and I knew I had to turn something else over to the Lord. "I'm willing to wait forever," I whispered, "but I want the right person to share my life with me, Lord. Someone who loves You first. Let him be the one You have for me or I want no one at all." At that moment I released whatever the days ahead might bring to the One who held my future in His hands.

With the end of the war, wild celebrations began in every city in the nation. Servicemen flooded the sidewalks and streets. Strangers were hugging each other and sobbing together. Gas rationing was discontinued immediately, and almost as suddenly scarce commodities were back on the market. Detroit was assuring the public that soon automobiles would be rolling from their assembly lines.

It was broadcast that Hitler had committed suicide. Slowly the nightmare of the concentration camps was discovered, horrors of the past years revealed atrocities that seemed unimaginable. It was as though the world had gone mad for four horrible years.

Now all of that was over. The Bomb had changed everything. Everyone wanted to forget as quickly as possible and pick up the pieces of their lives as they had been before the war. We were sure that we would never have to face such horrors again.

Enormous ships anchoring in harbors carried thousands of servicemen. Men were coming back to a different country than they had remembered, but it was home. Wives held their husbands close and parents wept on their sons' shoulders, while widows and other bereaved grieved quietly.

There was an air of expectancy and exhilaration. A new era was beginning, and I felt it especially as I left home for my last term at Moody. I could feel the excitement in the air, resounding in the airports, in taxicabs, on the streets. Servicemen were flooding the terminals, duffel bags swung over their shoulders, happy grins on their faces. The Allies had won the war, and victory made everyone proud.

My last semester was the best. By now Chicago had

become a way of life for me, and I felt at home. I knew I would miss the adventure of running through the railway stations, down the stairs into rumbling subways, or up to the crowded Els. The wind, the variety of seasons, and the diversity of people made Chicago a stimulating place to live. But in the middle of December the semester ended, and I had to say good-by to close friends and the city I had grown to love.

On the brief flight home I reread the letter I had received from my mother only that day. The words again brought tears to my eyes: "Do you remember Vern Johnson? His girl friend died suddenly a few weeks ago. After a sudden headache, she had a cerebral hemorrhage, and was gone within hours."

I thought of Vern with compassion. Recalling the intense loneliness I had felt in losing Tom, I knew what Vern must be going through now, and I breathed a prayer for him. I knew him briefly from church, and I remembered his girl friend, Diane, a tall, lovely girl. She and Vern had made quite a striking couple. But now she was gone. I promised myself that I would call him and offer my sympathy when I got home.

But once at home, I got caught up in getting resettled and somehow forgot about Vern for awhile. Nancy's fiancé, Steve, was home, and we were busy getting to know him. He entertained us for hours with stories of life in Africa and his war experiences. His wit enlivened the tales, though we knew he was concealing from us the pain of four years of loneliness and hardship. Steve and Nancy were rekindling their romance after their long separation and planned to be married in February.

Soon we were involved in the flurry of preparations for their wedding. There were gowns to fit, showers to give, and gifts to buy. Finally the night arrived. Nancy was a beautiful bride; Jennifer was maid-of-honor, proudly wearing a diamond of her own from her fiancé, Mike; I followed as bridesmaid. We three had been so close, and no one knew better than I that their friendship had found me just in time.

I could see a tear sliding down Jennifer's cheek, and my own eyes were filling as Nancy and Steve exchanged their vows.

We kissed Nancy good-by and waved them off on their honeymoon. Watching Nancy disappear in the car among the fullness of her satin wedding gown, I couldn't help but think how different things would be for us now. Our friendship would last forever, but it wouldn't be the same. I was so thankful for her friendship and how she had loved me into the kingdom of God. I longed for every moment of her life to be gloriously full.

Nancy had tossed her bridal bouquet right to me, her eyes twinkling, and I had caught it. I was still holding the flowers when Jennifer and I turned back to the reception. I caught a glimpse of Vern Johnson standing apart from the crowd. I hadn't expected to see him there, and I felt a pang of guilt for not calling him. He looked sad, but so darkly handsome that I caught my breath. I wanted to go and tell him how sorry I was about Diane, that I really did understand, but all I did was stand there looking at him when suddenly a question arose in my heart.

22

The roller-skating party for the college students was noisy and crowded, and when my friend Sharon and I joined the group I was almost sorry I had come. But it was Saturday night and better than staying home, so I began to renew acquaintances with the young people my age from church.

I stood at the rail, chin in hand, getting the feel of my skates and watching the whirling mass of skaters. Suddenly Vern Johnson appeared before my eyes, and just as suddenly he was gone, skating expertly through the crowds. I didn't hear Sharon skate up alongside me until she spoke. "I'd sure like to meet him. I wish he'd ask me to skate."

"Who?" I was jolted and looked at Sharon in surprise.

"Why, Vern Johnson, of course. He's good looking, don't you think?"

Before I could answer, I was skating away with Fred, but my eyes didn't stop searching for Vern. What was wrong with me anyway? I scolded myself. Around and around the floor Fred whirled me until I begged off and wandered to the snack bar.

The lights were dimming for the last round of the evening when there was Vern, his arm held out. He nodded toward the floor, and we silently wove our way through the couples. I wondered if the sound of my heart was drowning out the blaring organ. How did my answer come back so calm when he offered to take Sharon and me home?

Sharon lived farther away than I did, so I assumed he would take me home first, but we passed my street and took the highway to Sharon's house. After we dropped her off, Vern asked if I would like to stop for a cup of coffee. We did, and there our eyes met for the first time.

Words became sentences and stretched into a conversation that lasted into the early morning hours. Vern told me about the Sunday afternoon he and Diane had been out with friends and she had cried out, "Something's happening inside my head! I feel terrible!" He had driven her home, then rushed with her parents to the hospital. He shared with me the shock he and Diane's parents had received when the doctor informed them that Diane was dead. Then he paused, and I knew he was reliving the nightmare. Yet it seemed to be freeing to him to be able to talk with someone about the experience.

"It's impossible to believe that someone can be alive and laughing one hour and simply gone the next — just as if they had never been." He shook his head.

"Were you angry with God?" I asked gently.

"I was angry and hurt and couldn't believe it happened at all," he admitted. "But when I saw her, my anger melted away somehow. How can I explain it? It was like I knew Diane was with the Lord, whole and perfect. God's peace just flooded over me, and I felt He was telling me that all this was for some purpose that I couldn't understand now, but that good would come from it."

"And do you understand now?"

"Well, I understand one thing at least. Diane's father had been a nonbeliever, but now he has given his life to Christ. That's what Diane wanted most in the world to happen. This is what it took — ," Vern's eyes filled with tears, and he cleared his throat and turned his head.

Joy through sorrow. I remembered my mother's words long ago as she tried to explain to me that God was continually working *all* things together for good. I recalled how unhappy I had been when Tom was killed. I had had no comfort, no trust in a heavenly Father, only sorrow, anger, and self-pity. How different it was for Vern! For though he had loved and lost Diane, still he had peace. It *was* possible to walk through deep troubled waters and feel a kind of underlying joy and peace — something the world could never understand, for it only belonged to those who really believed God.

During the next quiet moments our hands met over the countertop, and we each found comfort in the touch. I felt content with him, a warmth I hadn't felt since I had lost Tom.

Every night for months, over endless cups of coffee, over candlelit dinners in small restaurants, driving on long stretches of highway and through wooded lanes, we grew closer. And before July had really settled in, Vern and I knew we were in love. The question in my heart had found its answer.

August arrived, and for my birthday Vern slipped a lovely diamond solitaire on my fourth finger. My parents grew to love Vern too, and mom and I began making preparations for a January wedding.

But there were some last-minute things I wanted to do to close an old chapter in my life. I visited Sherry's mother and told her about my faith in Jesus Christ. I told her that He alone could bring her the peace she needed since she had lost Sherry. She listened, rocking all the time, but when I left I knew that she hadn't heard me at all. Sherry had been her baby, the sunshine of her life. I walked down the wooden steps for the last time and whispered a final farewell to my friend and all the memories of long-ago days.

I wrote a lengthy letter to Kate, explaining to her about my changed life, but I didn't hear from her for a long time — and when she finally called me from the train station that day, she never mentioned the letter.

I went downtown to the square where all the names of the war dead from our town were engraved in marble. I found each name of the boys I had known, and my eyes rested for a long time on Tom's name.

"Good-by, dear Tom," I whispered and walked away.

The love of God had always been around me, but now I realized it completely. Looking back over the past few years, only divine love, only the love of a faithful heavenly Father, could have brought me from *there* to *here* — to this perfect moment of my life.

23

My wedding day arrived at last, bringing with it faint rays of sunshine through steadily falling snow. The snow ended by dusk, and as we left for the church the air was frosty and clear. Twinkling stars, enhancing the beauty of the night, filled the skies like thousands of diamonds strewn across dark velvet.

The evening was a beautiful dream-come-true. When the organ began to play quietly, my bridesmaid, Retha, Vern's sister, started down the aisle, her soft pastel gown a sunny contrast to the winter night. I felt especially blessed that she would be my new "sister." Jennifer was my maid-of-honor, looking elegant in lavender. She turned to smile at me before she preceded me down the aisle, and her eyes reflected my own happiness. I could see Nancy, just one month away from giving birth to their first child, near the front, aglow with happiness.

For an instant I remembered the night Nancy, Jennifer, and I had stood on the pier facing Lake Michigan and wondered about our futures. Our dreams had come true: we had longed for loving husbands and homes where God would be the honored Head; and because *He* had given us those desires, He fulfilled them.

Jennifer was almost to the altar now, and my moment had arrived. The organ rose to a great crescendo, and I placed my hand on my father's arm. Our guests rose to face us, but I saw only Vern, my bridegroom, waiting at the end of the aisle. He looked so tall and handsome in his tuxedo, and his smile was steady as he took my arm.

Dearly beloved.

Could this be the church I had avoided for so many years? Were these the people I had thought so cold and unfriendly? They truly were "dearly beloved," for there was a warmth as tangible as arms wrapping themselves sweetly about us.

We are gathered together in the sight of God.

At that moment I knew fully the difference God had made in my life. He had touched every area, transforming me into a new person. My attitudes, desires, friends, and hopes for the future had all been turned in His direction. He had led me to wonderful friends, to two years of study at a renowned Bible school, to a new relationship with my parents, and now to my beloved Vern. It was far more than I had hoped for or deserved.

For Thine is the kingdom, and the power, and the glory forever.

Vern and I knelt at the altar, my hand in his, as the words and music of "The Lord's Prayer" gloriously filled the sanctuary. In my heart were deep feelings of thankfulness and praise to God who had made all this possible.

And finally — *I now pronounce you husband and wife.*

Vern lifted my veil and our lips met. The Mendelssohn march began, and we walked down the aisle smiling at our "dearly beloved" friends and families.

Our wedding reception was held in the ornately beautiful Louis XV Room of a downtown hotel. Enormous chandeliers sparkled from the vast ceiling, illuminating the expansive room with a brilliant light. Vern and I sat with our wedding party at raised tables and smiled down at the hundreds of guests. I wanted to say something special to Vern — something simple and perfect — but he said it first: "Just think, honey, we have more than enough love to last all our lives."

We looked deep into each others' eyes, and the moment was sealed. For as long or as short as our life together might be, wherever God might lead us, we had taken our first step with a song of thanksgiving and praise on our lips.

Only God, my loving heavenly Father, could have chosen such a perfect life companion for me. And together we would have *more than enough love* from God Himself, the Source of love.

Would there be heartaches? Of course. But I would never again suffer as I had in the days when I floundered about in despair, not knowing God's peace. Now I knew that He would allow only those trials in our lives that would draw us nearer to Himself. His grace would be *more than enough* to carry us through any sorrow, for His word was sure: "(We) sorrow not as others who have no hope" (1 Thess. 4:13, author's paraphrase). Jesus would go through every trial with us, for He had promised, "I will never leave you, nor forsake you" (Heb. 13:5, author's paraphrase).

Joy? Always. We could plan on a lifetime of joy because our heavenly Father cared for our well-being more than we ourselves ever could. Christ had told His disciples: "My joy will be in you and your joy will be made full" (John 15:11, author's paraphrase). There would be *more than enough joy* in Christ, our Savior.

Children? We hoped so. With all our hearts we wanted to teach them to walk faithfully with the Lord. We would do this by the example of our own walk with Him and by our love for one another.

Security? Maybe not as the world counted security — no one had a blanket promise of safety from material loss — but we would be eternally secure in our Father's hand: "The steps of a man are established by the Lord; and He delights in his way. When he falls, he shall not be hurled headlong; because the Lord is the One who holds his hand" (Ps. 37:23,24 NAS).

Would we have arguments and disagreements? I knew myself too well to discount that possibility, but God was still "pruning" me, and I knew He would continue to chip away at my thorns and rough edges.

Would Vern love and cherish me as God commanded? Somehow my heart quietly confirmed that he would. And with such tender, caring love, could I not learn to be the kind of wife God intended me to be.

I smiled at my family, and they returned the smile with love. I winked at April, and she grinned back, bringing the faintest memory of the way Barry's eyes crinkled at the corners when he laughed. I remembered with thankfulness all my parents had taught me as a child, and I thought of the words of David: "The lines have fallen to me in pleasant places; indeed, my heritage is beautiful to me" (Ps. 16:6 NAS).

Smiling also at Vern's parents, I knew we were doubly blessed, for his heritage was beautiful also. We would have godly parents praying for us and for our children and perhaps for our children's children. We could pass on an eternal heritage with the promise: "But the lovingkindness of the Lord is from everlasting to everlasting on those who fear Him, and His righteousness to children's children" (Ps. 103:17 NAS).

There *was* something permanent in this life after all, and I knew what it was: "Christ in me, the hope of glory" (Col. 1:27, author's paraphrase). I remembered how I had knelt by my bed just a few short years before, sobbing to God for His forgiveness and guidance. Now I knew that every good thing that had happened to me since was a direct result of that decision.

Was God's love enough to keep us through the years ahead, to keep our love for each other warm and glowing? Yes, a thousand times, yes. It was *more than enough.*

For I was my Lord's, and He was mine.

I was my beloved bridegroom's, and he was mine.

Yes, we were together — forever — and had the beautiful promise of God's own love, joy, and peace. An inheritance that would be *more than enough* of everything we would ever need for all the days of our lives.

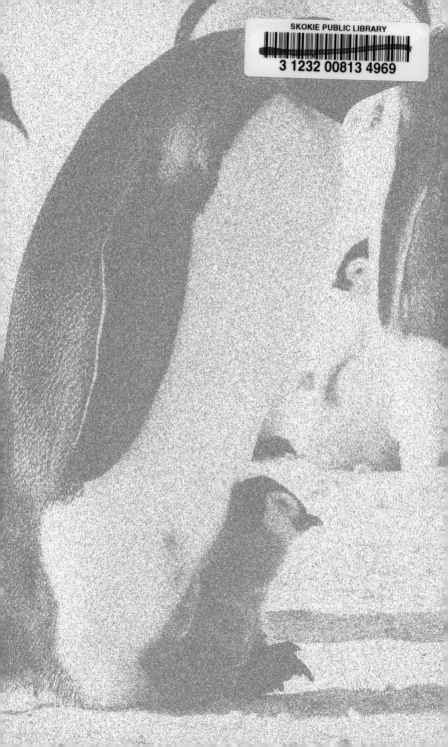